GW01463977

RELIGION, REASON AND THE SELF

ART and PHILOSOPHY
Contemporary Aesthetics

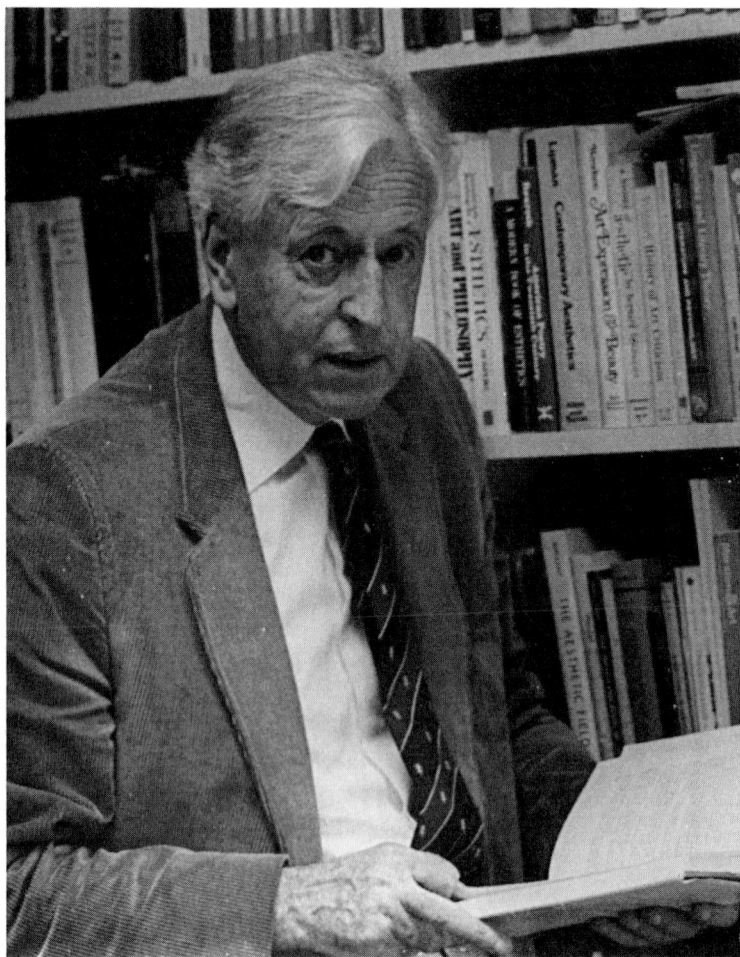

Hywel D. Lewis

RELIGION, REASON AND THE SELF

ESSAYS IN HONOUR OF HYWEL D. LEWIS

Edited by

Stewart R. Sutherland
T.A. Roberts

CARDIFF
UNIVERSITY OF WALES PRESS
1989

British Library Cataloguing in Publication Data

Religion, reason and the self, essays in honour
  of Hywel D. Lewis.
  1. Philosophy of religion
  I. Roberts, T.A. II. Sutherland, Stewart R.
  (Stewart Ross), *1941*
  III. Lewis, Hywel D. (Hywel David), *1910–*
  200′.1

ISBN 0-7083-1042-7

Printed in Great Britain at the Alden Press
Oxford London and Northampton

Contents

vi

The Contributors

Revd Professor **Frederick C. Copleston** is Emeritus Professor of Philosophy in the University of London. Before retiring in 1974, he was Principal of Heythrop College, University of London and in 1983 was Visiting Professor of Philosophy at Santa Clara University, California.

Dr **Meredydd Evans**, a former pupil of Hywel D. Lewis at the University College of North Wales, Bangor, was, before his retirement, on the staff of the Department of Extra Mural Studies, University College, Cardiff.

Professor **Ivor Leclerc** is Emeritus Professor of Philosophy, Emory University, Atlanta, Georgia, USA.

Professor **Thomas McPherson** is Emeritus Professor of Philosophy at University of Wales College of Cardiff. Before moving to Cardiff he was a colleague with Hywel D. Lewis in the Department of Philosophy at University College of North Wales, Bangor.

Revd Professor **H.P. Owen** is Emeritus Professor of Christian Doctrine in the University of London and a former colleague of Hywel D. Lewis in the Department of Religious Studies at King's College, London.

Professor **Dewi Z. Phillips** holds the Chair of Philosophy at the University College of Swansea.

Professor **T.A. Roberts** retired from the Chair of Philosophy at University College of Wales, Aberystwyth in 1988.

Professor **Stewart R. Sutherland** succeeded Hywel D. Lewis in the Chair of the History and Philosophy of Religion at King's College, University of London. He is at present Principal of

King's College and Vice-Chancellor elect of London University.

Professor **Richard Swinburne** was Professor of Philosophy in the University of Keele before his appointment to the Nolloth Chair of the Philosophy of the Christian Religion in the University of Oxford.

Very Reverend Professor **Thomas F. Torrance** is Emeritus Professor of Christian Dogmatics at the University of Edinburgh, having previously held the Chair of Church History at the same university.

Hywel D. Lewis

IT is fitting that this volume of tribute to Hywel David Lewis is published by the Press of the University of Wales, for Lewis is by birth, by nurture and by sensitivity a Welshman. He is, like the best of his fellow countrymen, international in his intellectual horizons, but he has drawn nourishment from his roots throughout his career.

These roots trace back to the place of his birth Llandudno in 1910. It is clear that he derived stimulus of mind and spirit from his early years as the son of the Presbyterian Minister of Waunfawr, which prepared him well to appreciate the opportunities offered by the Department of Philosophy at the University College of North Wales, Bangor. Of his teachers there, James Gibson, Gladys Lewis, Alan Stout, and C.A. Campbell, the most direct philosophical influence was probably Campbell, who ensured Lewis's respect for the earlier tradition of British idealism upon which they were both to draw selectively.

In Oxford he was fortunate to have close contact with two philosophers who later became distinguished academic statesmen, T.M. Knox, and Oliver (later, Lord) Franks. The philosophical strengths of Oxford were then great, and Lewis drank significantly, albeit selectively and critically, from the work of H.A. Prichard, W.D. Ross, and H.H. Price. Perhaps his independence of philosophical mind, for many his primary academic virtue, derives not only from his Welsh Presbyterian background, but also from the variety of themes and sympathies exemplified by his teachers.

He took the difficult decision to shorten his postgraduate course in Oxford in order to return to a lectureship in Bangor

and he remained there, becoming in due course Campbell's
successor in the Chair, until 1955. During this period he published six books in Welsh, and two in English. His Welsh
writings demonstrated an early interest and skill in writing
poetry, as well as wider philosophical and theological interests.
His two books in English, *Morals and the New Theology* (1947)
and *Morals and Revelation* (1951) helped consolidate a wider
philosophical reputation already established by a string of
articles in the major philosophical journals.

The marked, but by no means exclusive, interest in the
philosophy of religion again established him as a leading figure
in that field and he was appointed to the unique Chair of the
History and Philosophy of Religion in the University of
London. The Chair was shortly thereafter attached to King's
College London, and it was there that Lewis built an international reputation in the fields of the philosophy of religion
and the philosophy of mind. His range was of course much
wider than that as his writing and editorial activities demon-
strate well. However, his *Our Experience of God* (1959), and *The
Elusive Self* (Vol. I, 1969, and Vol. II, 1982) are regarded as
classic defenses of views which, more then than now, were
regarded as unfashionable.

Lewis's development as a philosopher of religion coincided
with, at times, quite severe pressure upon the subject, as often
ill-digested applications of the techniques of logical positivism
were used to constrain and corral the subject. The so-called
'linguistic' or 'analytical' philosophy dominated much of the
British scene. Although important contributions were made
from within that context, it fell to Lewis and a few others,
including some of his pupils, to retain an active seam of
thinking and writing which did justice to the wider perceptions
of the subject which a thorough grounding in its history justified.

Just as philosophy of religion had for some been conducted
upon an unduly limited agenda, so the influence of Ryle,
amongst others, seemed to have re-defined the acceptable limits
to discussion of topics within the philosophy of mind. Lewis did
not bow to such fashion and he has had the satisfaction of seeing
the reinstatement to the centre of the philosophical stage of
issues the importance of which he had consistently maintained.

However, the refusal to be diverted from what traditionally

have been understood as the central themes of philosophy and metaphysics — freedom and responsibility, the relationship of mind to body, the existence of God, reason and experience — has been recognized over the years in many ways by his peers. He is, I believe, alone in having held the Presidencies of The Mind Association, the Aristotelian Society *and* the Society for the Study of Theology. Amongst many other appointments, three of the most influential have been as Chairman of the Council of the Royal Institute of Philosophy, founding editor of the journal *Religious Studies* (1965–84), and President of the International Society of Metaphysics. He has been recognized outside his own native heath by the award of honorary degrees of the Universities of St Andrews, and Emory, Atlanta, USA.

He has travelled and lectured widely in this country and abroad. In addition to the Gifford Lectures (St. Andrews) and the Wilde Lectures (Oxford) he has given named lectures in Aberystwyth, Belfast, Birmingham, Nottingham and London in the United Kingdom, and McMaster and Toronto in Canada, Washington and Wheaton in the USA; and he delivered the Willer Lectures in Madras, a recognition of the very high reputation which his work has in the Indian subcontinent.

STEWART R. SUTHERLAND

UN a fagwyd yn Waunfawr, Arfon, yw'r gŵr y telir teyrnged iddo yn y gyfrol hon. Byddai peidio â chynnwys ei briod iaith ynddi yn chwithdod yn ei olwg ac yn ddiffyg o safle'r sawl a ŵyr rywfaint am deithi meddwl Cymru Gymraeg y ganrif hon. Cyfrannodd Hywel D. Lewis yn helaeth i drafodaethau athronyddol, diwinyddol, cymdeithasol a diwylliannol ei bobl a hynny, yn ddieithriad, mewn Cymraeg graenus, clir.

O'r cychwyn cyntaf ni allai fod amheuaeth ynglŷn â gradd y gwreiddyn oedd iddo. Cafodd hwnnw bridd rhywiog ar aelwyd a chymdeithasau bro ei febyd, gyda dylanwad ei dad yn neilltuol o gryf arno. Roedd ef yn fathemategwr dawnus a wnaeth enw iddo'i hun yng Nghaer-grawnt. Pwyswyd arno yno gan rai o'i athrawon i ymroi yn llwyr i waith prifysgol ond dewisodd yn hytrach fywyd gweinidog gyda'r Hen Gorff, yn Llandudno i ddechrau ac yna yn Waunfawr lle treuliodd ddeugain mlynedd ffrwythlon yn was cydwybodol i'w Arglwydd. Yn ystod ei oes casglodd lyfrgell gampus gyda lle teilwng, bid siwr, i fathemateg ar ei silffoedd ond bod yr wyddor honno, yn ei thro, yn gorfod ildio lle amlycach i ddiwinyddiaeth a llenyddiaeth Gymraeg a Saesneg. Porfa fras i blentyn llengar a manteisiodd Hywel, a'i frawd Alun, yn barod arni.

At hyn cawsant ddigonedd o gyfle i wrando ar sgwrsio a thrafod bywiog, deallus, rhwng eu rhieni a'r mynych gyfeillion a chydnabod a ymwelai â'r aelwyd. Ymunent hwythau'r bechgyn, o bryd i'w gilydd, yn y trafod. Yn wir, bu Hywel yn ddigon eofn sawl tro i dynnu torch ag ambell weinidog a bregethai am bechod gwreiddiol, anorfod; hyn â chryn anghysur i'w fam ond â pheth difyrrwch i'w dad. Yr un oedd y llanc hwn, yn y dyddiau cynnar hynny, â'r athronydd a luniodd, yn ddiweddarach, ddadleuon *Morals and the New Theology*. Dyna fel y disgrifiodd ef, yn un o'i ysgrifau, ei gefndir teuluol a brodorol:

> Speculation and argument was in the air we breathed, and we had much of this in the services and bible classes too.

Gwir mai ym Mangor yr aeth i'r afael yn ffurfiol ag athroniaeth am y tro cyntaf ond bwriodd brentisiaeth werth chweil yn y cartref yn Arfon.

Saesneg, wrth gwrs, oedd iaith athronyddu yn y coleg ond erbyn iddo raddio yn 1932 roedd Adran Athronyddol Urdd y Graddedigion bron yn flwydd oed a chyfle iddo yntau, felly, wrth gynadleddu unwaith y flwyddyn o leiaf, drin a thrafod ei ddewis bynciau ag eraill o gyffelyb fryd. Dylid cofio hefyd fod nifer sylweddol o ymgeiswyr am y weinidogaeth yng ngholegau Bangor y pryd hwnnw ac nad oedd prinder trafodaethau athronyddol a diwinyddol Gymraeg ymhlith y rhai mwyaf bywiog ohonynt. Erbyn 1938 roedd yn aelod o Fwrdd Golygyddol *Efrydiau Athronyddol* a diamau mai bodolaeth yr Adran hon a'i chylchgrawn a fu'r prif ysgogiad iddo athronyddu yn Gymraeg.

Cyhoeddodd nifer o lyfrau ar destunau athroniaeth crefydd (*Gwybod am Dduw*, 1952 a *Pwy yw Iesu Grist?*, 1979); athroniaeth gwleidyddiaeth (*Gweriniaeth*, 1940 ac *Y Wladwriaeth a'i Hawdurdod*, 1943, yr olaf ar y cyd â J. Alun Thomas); astudiaethau diwylliannol a chymdeithasol (*Diogelu Diwylliant*, 1945, a *Dilyn Crist*, 1951). Cafwyd ganddo hefyd bamffled ar un o faterion dwysaf y dydd, *Crist a Heddwch* (1947) a llyfr taith, *Hen a Newydd* (1971), yn cynnwys cryn lawer o fyfyrio ar grefyddau'r India. Cyfrannodd nifer o erthyglau i'r cylchgronau Cymraeg ar amryw bynciau yn ogystal â chyhoeddi cyfrol o farddoniaeth, *Ebyrth* (1943). A rhag inni dybio ei fod yn amddifad o ddigrifwch ac ysmaldod iach, y flwyddyn ddiwethaf (1988) cyhoeddodd gasgliad o rigymau dan y pennawd *Gofidiau Patsi*, am dreialon ac anturiaethau gast fach a berthynai iddo pan fu'n byw ym Mangor.

Am yn agos i chwarter canrif bu'n ddarlithydd ac yna yn Athro yng Ngholeg y Gogledd, Bangor, gan ddylanwadu yn drwm ar nifer fawr o fyfyrwyr. Darlithiai yn drefnus, yn hyfryd o glir, ac i'r sawl a fynnai drafod problemau athronyddol y tu allan i'r ystafell ddarlithio nid oedd yn grintach â'i amser. Roedd ganddo ddiddordeb dwfn mewn addysg oedolion a dar-lithiai'n fynych i sawl cymdeithas a sefydliad Cymraeg. Bu'n pregethu ac yn annerch droeon yng nghyfarfodydd ei enwad, a safodd yn gadarn dros egwyddorion heddychaeth Gristnogol mewn sawl cyfarfod cyhoeddus. Fel un a fagwyd mewn ardal chwarelyddol bu ganddo ddiddordeb arbennig yn Undeb Chwarelwyr Gogledd Cymru.

Yn 1955 fe'i penodwyd i Gadair Hanes ac Athroniaeth Crefydd Coleg y Brenin, ym Mhrifysgol Llundain, ac yno, am dros chwarter canrif arall, bu'n rhyfeddol o gynhyrchiol gan ymsefydlu yn ffigur cydwladol ym maes athroniaeth crefydd. Eto, er ei holl deithio tramor a'i ymroddiad i'w Adran trwy ei chysylltu â phrif ganolfannau astudiaethau crefydd ym mhedwar ban byd, cadwodd a meithrinodd gysylltiadau clos â'i wlad a'i genedl.

Bu Prifysgol Cymru, a'i swyddogaeth arbennig fel prifysgol genedlaethol, yn fater o'r pwys mwyaf iddo gydol y blynydd-oedd. Fel y datganodd yn *Diogelu Diwylliant* priod waith prif-ysgol yw 'cyfryngu i gymdeithas mewn amgylchiadau neilltuol yr hyn sydd yn gyffredinol yn niwylliant y byd', a dadleuodd yn gyson na ellid gwneud hynny yn briodol ym Mhrifysgol Cymru heb roi lle allweddol ynddi i weinyddu a hyfforddi trwy gyfrwng y Gymraeg. Cryfhaodd ei bwyslais ar hyn gyda'r blynyddoedd trwy ei waith fel Warden Urdd y Graddedigion, aelod o Lys y Brifysgol ac, yn neilltuol, o Lys ei hen goleg ei hun ym Mangor. Bu'n ddiflino, a phriodol hallt yn aml, yn ei feirniadaeth o'r Brifysgol ar y mater arbennig hwn. Mater o ofid i lu o'i gyfeillion a'i gydnabod, ac o gywilydd i Brifysgol ei wlad, yw na welodd honno'n dda i'w anrhydeddu am ei gyfraniadau iddi hi, i'w genedl ac i'r byd athronyddol yn gyffredinol. Bu'n ddiwyro yn ei ffyddlondeb i sefydliadau crefyddol a diwylliannol Cymru. Ni phallodd yn ei ymwneud â hwy ond parhaodd i annerch mewn llu o'u cyfarfodydd, yn eglwysi, colegau, ysgolion, cymdeithasau, eisteddfodau, ac ati. Bu'n ymwelydd cyson â'r Eisteddfodau Cenedlaethol yn arbennig ac y mae'n ddarllenydd brwd o'r wasg newyddiadurol Gymraeg a Chymreig. Go brin bod unrhyw ddigwyddiad o bwys ym mywyd gwleidyddol a chymdeithasol Cymru sy'n dianc rhag ei sylw. Tyst o hynny yw'r llythyrau mynych a anfonir ganddo i'r cylchgronau a'r newyddiaduron.

Ni bu neb yn fwy teyrngar nag ef i Adran Athronyddol Urdd y Graddedigion, a phrin iawn yw nifer y cynadleddau a drefnwyd ganddi y methodd ef â bod yn bresennol ynddynt. A bod yn dreiddgar bresennol ynddynt, sylwer. Heb fod ag ofn angerdd arno. Nid ar chwarae bach yr ymeflir codwm ag ef ar faterion athronyddol.

Mewn llythyr at gyfaill mynegodd Henry Jones mai'r hyn a wnaeth yn ei ddarlithoedd Gifford ef, *A Faith that Enquires*, oedd torri ei 'gŵys unig ei hun'. Gellir dweud yn gyffelyb am Hywel D. Lewis. Gyda doniau meddyliol disglair a dycnwch anarferol mae wedi trin ei dir heb ddibrisio ffasiynau athronyddol ei gyfnod ond eu mesur a'u pwyso yng ngoleuni ei ddealltwriaeth ei hun o draddodiadau athronyddol yr oesoedd. Iddo ef bu athronyddu, nid yn gymaint yn fodd i fyw, ond yn ffordd o fyw.

MEREDYDD EVANS

Meaning in the Bible

RICHARD SWINBURNE

CHRISTIAN orthodoxy has with various degrees of emphasis and qualification claimed that the Bible is true. It contains the crucial elements of Christian revelation and forms a touchstone by which doctrinal claims may be tested. I wish to apply philosophical understanding of meaning to inquire what it would be like for the Bible to be true. It will turn out that the answer depends on whether the Bible is one book or many, and on who is its author and its intended audience. This chapter is offered in grateful appreciation of Hywel Lewis's encouragement of the philosophy of religion in Great Britain, and of his contribution to it.

I

Truth belongs initially to token sentences, i.e. particular utterances or inscriptions on particular occasions.[1] What a given type of sentence 'The king is coming' or 'I am ill' asserts on an occasion of its utterance or inscription depends crucially on outside factors of two kinds. First and obviously, its meaning depends on the rules of the language in which it was uttered — the rules of syntax, and the semantic rules which give sense to the individual words. I shall say no more about that obvious point. But secondly the meaning of the token sentence depends on the context in which it was uttered. By the context I mean both the social context (who said it, when, to whom, after what, etc.) or, in the case of a written sentence, the literary context (the surrounding sentences of the letter or book, and the author, intended audience, and time of writing) *and* the cultural context (the beliefs common in the immediate group and the wider society in which the sentence was uttered, and the society's conventions for understanding words spoken and written in certain kinds of context). (I shall sometimes write merely 'uttered' instead of 'uttered or written', and more generally for simplicity's sake make remarks only about spoken sentences which are intended to apply to written ones as well, or vice versa. It will be clear how to extend them to the other case.) The social (or written) context provides reference for the terms. The meaning of 'I am ill' depends on the reference of 'I' and therefore on who is the speaker; and of 'what you just said is false' depends on who is the hearer and on what he has said. The cultural context is crucial for meaning in a number of ways. First, the cultural context of common beliefs (together with the social context) is necessary in order to understand any metaphorical use of words. What is obviously (to speaker and intended audience) false must be taken metaphorically.[2] I say, as John comes into the room, 'Here comes Ronald Reagan'. The obvious falsity of what I say, taken literally, suggests that we look for another meaning. We do this by looking for features commonly associated with Ronald Reagan such that the ascription of these to John would be appropriate in the context of the conversation. If the conversation has been about the fact that, although John is a friendly man, he has recently made a speech advocating reintroduction of the death penalty (social context), then the common belief of society that Reagan is a popular, friendly conservative, an actor who appeals to gut old-fashioned attitudes with no sensitivity to liberal values or the subtleties of issues (cultural context) shows what I mean when I say 'Here comes Ronald Reagan'; I mean that John is like Reagan in these respects. Secondly, cultural context of literary conventions is crucial for understanding which parts of a literary work are to be taken as asserted by its author, and among those which are to be taken literally and which metaphorically. A written sentence gains its meaning from its place within a written work (literary context) and the conventions of the society in which it was written for understanding a work of that genre. Literary works belong to different genres. We classify a work as belonging to a given genre by the similarity of its form and the relations of its sentences to the world and to other contemporary works. A contemporary work is a work of science fiction in virtue of the kind of plot it has and the way readers understand its sentences (as fiction), which is similar to that of a whole host of contemporary works and which we classify together as belonging to the same genre. The genre determines how a sentence which belongs to a work of that genre is to be taken, whether it has a truth-value, and, if so, whether it is to be taken literally or metaphorically. If 'Larry is an elephant' occurs in a children's story, it has no truth-value. If it occurs in a guidebook to the London Zoo, it does and is to be taken literally; the genre rules out the possibility of metaphor. But if it occurs in a poem, metaphorical meaning is always a serious possibility, to be adopted if a literal meaning is in any way unlikely.

We may wish to make a distinction between two elements in the meaning of token-sentences — what is said and what is presupposed — and to say that truth-value belongs only to what is said and not to the presuppositions in terms of which it is cast. Philosophers have most usually discussed this question in connection with referring expressions, that is, expressions such as proper names ('John') or definite descriptions ('The Prime Minister') which purport to pick out individual objects in order to say something about them, e.g., 'John is old'. It is the presupposition of sentences containing referring expressions that there exists an object picked out by that expression. Now suppose, to use an example much discussed in philosophical literature, I am at a party and note a man in the corner, drinking what I take to be martini, being very cheerful. I say to my companions 'The man drinking martini is very cheerful'. However, the man to whom I was intending to refer was not drinking martini, but sherry. Is what I have said true, false, or neither? Contemporary philosophers are divided on this issue. Some, following Russell,[3] claim that what I have said is false. For what I have said is analysable as 'There is a man drinking martini and he is very cheerful', and since the first conjunct is false the whole is false. Others, following Strawson,[4] claim that it is neither true nor false, for since the referring expression fails to refer, there is nothing for what I say to be true or false about. Yet others may plausibly claim that if the context makes clear to whom I am intending to refer and what I say applies to him, then what I have said is true.[5] It seems to me, however, that our

ordinary use of 'true' and 'false' is, in general, simply not precise
enough for there to be an obvious right answer to the question
of whether what is said is true, false, or neither in such cases
where the referring expression fails to refer.[6] However, although
the answer is not obvious in the case where the speaker alone
has the false belief that his description applies to his intended
referent, it does begin to seem fairly obvious that if public
criteria make clear to what an intended reference is being
made, the fact that it is made by means of a false description
does not make false what is said about the referent when the
false description embodies the presuppositions of a whole
culture. Roman historians may record the deeds of 'the divine
Augustus'. Must we judge as false all the details of his life which
they give because we think that no Augustus was 'divine'?
Biographers tell us mundane details of the life of Gautama ('the
Buddha'); if they tell us that 'the enlightened one' did this or
that, do we judge as false what they say if we think that
Gautama was not at all 'enlightened'? The answer in these
cases, intuitively, is surely 'No'. The same goes for examples in
the history of science. Some detailed eighteenth-century 'discovery' about 'dephlogisticated air', true of oxygen, would not
be said to be false just because there is no phlogiston. A more
natural description of what had happened would be that a true
discovery was made, but it was expressed in terms of a false
presupposition (that what we call 'oxygen' is ordinary air from
which phlogiston has been subtracted). A number of writers
recently[7] have claimed that scientific progress involves adding
to the stock of true sentences; that we think that science has
made gradual progress over the past two millenia, that in
consequence we must think of earlier science as achieving some
true results; and slightly later science as achieving a few more;
and that to think thus we must suppose that earlier scientists
were talking about many of the same entities as we do and that
progress consisted in adding to the stock of true information
about those entities; and that would involve supposing that
those entities were formerly picked out by false descriptions. If
you suppose that something is known about an object (e.g.,
electricity) only when you have a fully true description of its
nature or effects by which to pick it out, little would have been
discovered by scientists, the argument goes, until the last
century and a half.

This argument is questionable, for maybe progress involves not adding to the stock of true sentences, but replacing false sentences by other false sentences which approximate better to the truth. In any case neither these writers nor any others seem to me to bring out the main reason for saying that the falsity of the description in a referring expression does not, so long as the context makes clear what is the referent, affect the truth-value of the sentence. That reason is this. By a sentence such as 'The divine Augustus travelled to Brindisi', written in the course of conveying other detailed historical information, a Roman historian is seeking to add to his readers' stock of information. He would regard himself as having succeeded if they then came to believe that Augustus travelled to Brindisi, whether or not they shared his view that Augustus was divine. That that is what is crucial in the utterance of the sentence would be a view held not merely by the individual speaker but by others of his culture; they would see that as the job of the sentence in that location. The writer and his hearers would see the sentence as false if Augustus did not travel to Brindisi. If we judge it as false if either Augustus was not divine or he did not travel to Brindisi, we may judge it as false in respect of an aspect quite other than writers and immediate readers would have judged as part of his message. We would have imposed our categories of 'true' and 'false' upon the sentence in virtue of truth-conditions which the speaker and its culture would not have regarded as relevant to its message, and which therefore public criteria would not pick out as relevant. We would thus be ignoring the close tie to which H.P. Grice drew our attention, between the meaning of a sentence and the belief which, other things being equal, speakers use the sentence to instil. Our account of what made the sentence true or false would not be one sensitive to the whole of the sentence in the circumstances of its utterance.

But if falsity of description of a referent does not destroy the reference or the truth of what is said about it, so long as there are public criteria for what the referent is, the same should apply to any other elements presupposed in the sentence in terms of which its message is cast. I say, pointing to some water, 'That is a very beautiful river', but what I point to is not a river, but a lake. It is nevertheless a beautiful stretch of water. True, false, or neither? I say 'Jane opened the door for her father'. I say that because I believe that the man in whose house Jane lived was the father; but he is not, he is only her stepfather. She nevertheless opened the door for him. Is what I have said true, false, or neither? The answer again becomes more obvious when we consider cases where the presuppositions are those of a whole culture, and where there are public criteria for distinguishing those elements of a sentence which are irrelevant to its message from those which are not. I end my biography of Brown by saying that he 'fell asleep' or 'joined the spirits of his ancestors'. The point of my remark is not to make a theological claim, but to make a biographical one about the date of Brown's death. To assess the remark for truth-value it is not necessary to have a view about the afterlife. Again, the reason is that apportionment to a sentence of truth-value ought to be sensitive to the information that the sentence seeks to convey, not to the way in which it is expressed. For inevitably when I attempt to tell you something quickly, I rely on common assumptions as much as I can in order to convey the new message. To criticize the information we must separate it from the assumptions.

This is not always easy, but it can be done. The criteria for meaning and truth-value must be public. For what we are assessing is not the agent's intention, but the worth of what he publicly said. We must ask, whatever the agent's actual beliefs, what were the common beliefs of the culture which the agent would reasonably have presupposed to be shared with him in the community; and whatever the actual purpose of his utterance, can any presupposed beliefs be siphoned off, leaving what we can reasonably suppose to be the main message intact? If they can, we must then judge the truth-value of the utterance by criteria to which the falsity of the presuppositions is irrelevant. What determines the truth or falsity of 'Brown fell asleep in AD 1650', as uttered in seventeenth-century England, is not whether death is a temporary sleep, but only whether Brown died in 1650. Cultural context is thus crucial for how the message/presupposition distinction is to be drawn.

The meaning of a sentence being a public thing, it is, we have seen, the social and cultural context which determines the meaning of what is said, not the intention. I may say 'you are gauche', intending thereby to say that you are left wing; but the meaning of what I actually say is that you are clumsy. But there are limits to the extent to which a sentence uttered by a speaker can have a sense quite other than that which he intends. For the speaker's capacities and system of beliefs determine to which cultural context his utterances belong. If I utter a Japanese sentence which sounds the same as some English sentence, the meaning of what I have said is the meaning of the English sentence, not the Japanese. This is because I do not speak Japanese. And if a two-year-old says of some gorilla 'That's my father', he does not mean by it the metaphorical assertion which would be made by a speaker familiar with the theory of evolution. For his beliefs are so remote from those of the contemporary scientifically educated community that his utterance is not to be judged by their presuppositions. The language which determines the meaning of what is said must be known to the speaker, and the context must be one readily accessible to the speaker; he may have mistaken beliefs about it, but the true beliefs must be, as it were, within his range. Any context or language other than one available to the speaker will not give the meaning of the sentence as uttered by that speaker. Someone in the sixteenth century who says 'One day flying saucers will land on earth' does not utter a sentence with the meaning which we would ascribe to it if it were uttered today.

The social context of a sentence may not be fully known to a speaker's contemporaries and, for that reason, they may fail to understand the sentence; but its meaning is what (with their cultural assumptions shared with the speaker) they would judge it to be if they did know its context. A poem written about a land which the poet has seen but we have not, may use metaphors whose sense will only be apparent to those familiar with the land. Indeed, in ignorance of the land we may not understand that the poem is about it. Before we can understand the poem we have to know the context, and that means sharing the beliefs which would be generated by familiarity with the land.

So the truth of a sentence depends crucially on the context in which it is uttered; on who is the author, of what work the sentence is a part, and when and where that work is produced. For a longer work the truth of the whole will normally depend on the truth of its constituent sentences. For most genres (be they works of history, philosophy, or physics) the whole is true if and only if each constituent indicative (unquoted) sentence is true; to the extent to which it contains false sentences, it is not completely true. (If a sentence is quoted, its truth-value is irrelevant to the truth-value of the whole. What is relevant is whether the speaker (writer) said to have uttered (written) that sentence did so.) In a work of fiction or a poem, most of the sentences do not have a truth-value, and even if some do so (as when a historical novel includes some true history), their truth-value is not relevant to the truth of the whole. In general, works of fiction or poetry are not true or false; but if they have any evident message detectable by public criteria, they may be described as 'true' in so far as that message is true. Thus, parables commending some sort of conduct or poems depicting some features of a situation may be judged as true even though their constituent sentences are not all true. In general, however, parables and plays, dialogues, novels and poems are more properly assessed as 'illuminating', 'inspiring', 'profound', etc., rather than as 'true' or 'false'.

II

The Bible is a big book, composed of many smaller books, themselves woven together out of yet smaller strands of writing, with a different social and cultural context and a different literary context (embedded in a different religious work) at each stage of its production and subsequent use. The meaning of any sentence within it will therefore depend on which larger unit it is thought of as belonging to; and also on who is the author of that unit.

So let us begin by going back to the smallest units, the bits of poetry and story and oracle from various sources from which the books of the Bible were put together — those units which do not contain any smaller units which had any life of their own in speech or writing. It was form criticism which drew our attention to these smallest units. The Bible scholar, inspired by this movement, seeks to isolate each smallest unit and ask of it what did it mean when it was originally used, orally, or, as the case may be, in writing? To answer this the scholar must locate the original social context and the original cultural context (discover the common beliefs of the society). He must identify the unit as belonging to a genre and show how units of that genre are used. Discovering social and cultural context is not easy, and the results of biblical scholars in this area are somewhat speculative. But their problem is a soluble one, and in so far as they can solve it, they can tell us the meaning of the unit as originally used.

The social context will reveal the reference of the terms. If Psalm 21 was originally used as a hymn in a New Year festival for the enthronement of the King in the first Temple, then we know to whom 'the king' refers — the king currently being enthroned. The cultural context enables us to recognize and interpret any metaphorical use of words. Consider Rev.1:8, 'I am the Alpha and the Omega, saith the Lord God'. Taken literally, God is making a claim to be identical with two different Greek letters. The obvious falsity of what is said directs us to a metaphorical interpretation.[8] For this we look to beliefs common in the society — that alpha is the first letter of the alphabet and omega the last. The firstness of alpha and the lastness of omega suggest that what is being said is that God claims to be the first thing on which other things depend and after which they follow; and that the final purpose of things depends on their relation to God, who will determine what ultimately happens to them.

Knowledge of the cultural context will enable us to recognize instances of different literary genres and thus to see to what extent the truth-value of the whole is a function of the truth-value of its constituent sentences. However, the literary genres to which biblical units belong are ones unfamiliar to modern men. To detect the literary genre we must compare the unit in question with similar units of Middle Eastern literature, and see how these functioned in the society. Much more hard work by biblical scholars is necessary before we can be reasonably sure which genres have truth-value and what are the criteria for their truth, and maybe we can never make more than a reasonable guess at this. Thus biblical scholars dispute whether a parable has an allegorical interpretation (i.e., whether each referring term, predicate, etc., of each parable has an interpretation peculiar to that context) for example, that in the parable of the Sower (Mark 4: 3–9) Jesus is the sower, the 'seed'

is the gospel message, and so on.[9] If so, individual sentences of
a parable will have a truth-value. Alternatively, the parable as
a whole may have a truth-value, though individual sentences
do not. Or, finally, the parable may not have a truth-value at
all, merely be 'inspiring' or 'deep'.

Even when and if we are clear about the truth-criteria of
different biblical genres, it is often far from clear to which genre
a particular unit belongs; and again, much scholarly work is
required to answer such questions. Isaiah 5: 1–7 is an obvious
parable, but what of Daniel 6 (the story of Daniel and his
friends in the burning fiery furnace)? Is this supposed to be a
true historical record, or is it a parable? If the latter, does it
have an obvious message which can be assessed as true, or is
even this inappropriate? Locating a sentence as part of a hymn
means that it is only to be assessed as true or false in so far as
it contributes to the theological message of the hymn; the latter
alone is true or false. If the hymn 'There is a green hill far away'
is to have a truth-value, it is not one which is affected by
discovering that the Hill of Calvary is normally brown and the
hymn was originally used in Israel. And so likewise with Psalm
105, an obvious hymn. Verse 18 reports of the captured Joseph:
'His feet they hurt with fetters; he was laid in chains of iron.'
Genesis does not give explicitly these details of Joseph's im-
prisonment. But it is obviously irrelevant to the truth of the
psalm whether he was bound with chains of iron, or some other
metal, or rope. But whether he was imprisoned at all is, I
suggest, relevant to the truth. Crucial issues, however, concern
which biblical units are hymns in this respect. My view is that
Genesis 1 is a hymn; in that case, dates and order are no more
relevant to its truth than they are for 'All things bright and
beautiful'.

Another important kind of unit on which the Bible, and especially the Old Testament, is built, is the prophecy; and which
modern genre is closest to the genre of biblical prophecy is not at
all clear. The crucial issue is, was a 'prophecy' intended to be
unconditional (this is what will happen, whatever you do) or
conditional (this is what will happen unless you do something to
stop it)? Twentieth-century prophecies of political disaster
sometimes have an unexpressed clause ('unless you do something
about it') and there is plenty of evidence internal to the Old

Testament that biblical prophecies were normally so understood[10] (but not always). Again, how we are to understand
Jeremiah's prophecy to Zedekiah (on behalf of the Lord), (Jer:
33.17f.) — 'David shall never want a man to sit on the throne of
the house of Israel; neither shall the priests, the Levites, want a
man before me to offer burnt offerings, and to burn oblations and
to do sacrifice' — depends on whether we are to regard it as false
if and only if there is no king of Israel or the priests do not
continue to do sacrifice, or as false if and only if these things do not
happen even though Israel behaves well.

Cultural context is also crucial for distinguishing what is said
from the presuppositions in terms of which it is cast. The
sentences of the Bible often have false scientific or historical
presuppositions. They often, for example, presuppose that the
earth is flat, square and stationary, covered with a dome across
which the sun, moon and stars travel by day and night. But the
cultural context reveals these as common presuppositions of the
society, and the social context typically reveals the main
message as not to communicate these but something else by
means of them. The falsity of the presuppositions does not,
therefore (by my earlier argument), affect the truth-value of
the sentence which uses them. Psalm 104 praises God for many
marvels of nature including that 'he laid the foundations of the
Earth, that it should not be moved forever' (104:5). Now the
earth has no 'foundations' in some other body, which was what
the psalmist supposed. But what he was getting at was that the
earth is not wobbly, you can build on it, it is firm; and he
expressed the claim that God is responsible for this, using the
presuppositions of his culture. If God is indeed responsible for
this stability, the sentence is true. Genesis 8:2 tells us that at the
end of the Flood 'the windows of heaven were stopped'. Heaven
has no windows out of which the rain comes, but the quoted
sentence is just the author's way of saying, within the presuppositions of his culture, that the rain ceased. If it did, the
sentence is true.

So much for the criteria of truth of the smallest units of the
Bible as originally uttered or written. But compilers put the
units together into larger units with the addition of connecting
verses until we have whole strands, such as the J, E, D and P
sources in the Pentateuch, having continuity and unity. These

were put together into the Books of the Old and New Testaments as we know them. And then the books of the Old
Testament were gradually recognized as a canonical collection,
and to them were added by the Christian Church the books of
the New Testament which were given a similar status.

Units change their meaning when inserted into larger
wholes. Secular books today are not in general formed in the
patchwork way in which the Bible was formed, but there are
some simple modern examples of how the literary context
changes the meaning. First, of course, speeches and documents
are quoted verbatim. The original production of the speech
expressed certain views; its quotation merely claims that those
words were uttered. Secondly, a preface or appendix may be
added in which explicitly or by implication the author states
that he no longer affirms some of the contents, or that he wishes
them to be understood in some unusual way. For an example
of a preface which did this covertly, consider Osiander's preface
to Copernicus's *De Revolutionibus*, saying that this detailed work
which asserted that the earth went round the sun and thereby
enabled detailed calculations of planetary positions to be made,
was to be read not as claiming that the earth did go round the
sun but simply as saying that this assumption was useful for
making predictions. Thirdly, a footnote may correct something
in the text, saying that it is to be understood in some unusual
way.

These three changes to the meaning of units involve no
tampering with the text, only a different understanding given
to those words by the literary context. In so far as modern works
are formed by cobbling together earlier units, words may be
changed to make the units consistent or to have a different
overall message, in such a way as radically to change the
meaning of the unit. The most usual modern example of this is
where one author puts together separate papers of his or her
own to make a book, and changes some of the sentences especially of earlier papers to make the whole mutually consistent.
Although there must be few examples in modern literature of
a whole formed by sewing together units of some antiquity
written by different authors and groups, the examples from
modern literature will illustrate what happens to the meaining
of the units under these circumstances.

We can see all of this happening in the formation of the books of the Bible. The process of quotation is of course apparent everywhere. Thus the prophetic books contain 'oracles', namely, separate speeches, which are in the edited book said to have been spoken by (for example) Jeremiah at a certain place (Jer. 7:1f.). In the case of the Bible, however, the process of quotation seldom makes any differences to what is asserted, since almost the only speakers quoted are those supposed to be inspired to speak the truth, and so ones whose speeches are endorsed by the compiler. There are, however, biblical examples where the addition of a preface or appendix changes the whole tone of the book. The whole tone of the book of Ecclesiastes is changed by the addition of certain verses, especially at the end (12:13f.), which purport to summarize its message but really give it a radically new look. A sceptical book becomes a God-centred book. But, as with the Osiander preface, if we take the whole book including that preface, that's the way the book is to be read — that's the meaning it has when that preface is seen as an integral part of it.

Footnotes are not a device known to ancient writers. Their substitute for a correcting or amplifying footnote is a verse correcting the previous verse, or a connecting verse saying that the next paragraph fills out the previous one. Daniel 12:12. seems to be a verse correcting the previous verse in respect of the number of days until the 'end'. An interesting example of a connecting verse is Genesis 2:4a. This has the function, according to B.S. Childs,[11] of explaining that the narrative of Genesis 2, which in various ways contradicts that of Genesis 1 (one example is that plants seem to be created before man in Genesis 1, but after man in Genesis 2 — see Gen. 2:5, 7 and 9) is to be read as a detailed filling out in some respects of Genesis 1.

Correction of verses so as to make the whole consistent or to have a different message is not a process which is obvious unless we have the original, and it is most in evidence in the corrections to St Mark (or his source) made in the Gospels of St Matthew and St Luke (e.g. the insertion of the clause 'except for fornication' in Matthew 19:9. Matthew 19: 3–11 seems to derive from Mark 10: 2–12). Sometimes the correction seems to derive from a misunderstanding of the original, for example by taking literally what was not meant to be taken too literally (e.g. Matthew taking literally Mark's report that at the Crucifixion 'the veil of the temple was rent in twain from the top to the bottom'[12]).

Changing the context of the units and sewing them together into a literary work has different effects in different places. One interesting example concerns the psalms. Many of them originally had a cultic context (in the rituals of the first temple) which is lost when they come to form a collection of hymns for private or synagogic use. The compiler of the Book of Psalms must have supposed many of the psalms to have meanings (e.g. as expressions of personal devotion) other than their original meaning).

Just as the genre of the individual unit is hard for the modern reader to recognize, so is the genre of the biblical book. In my view the books of Ruth and Jonah are parables; and these parables do not have a truth which consists in the correspondence of each of their sentences to historical facts.[13] But they are easy cases, and the conventions of other books of the Old and New Testaments are much more difficult to detect. Job and 2 Esdras are obviously concerned with the problem of evil, but are they treatises which seek to provide a theodicy, or works which seek to stimulate the philosophical imagination, or works which record the story and perplexity of particular individuals? In the first and third cases their truth-value is a function of the truth-value of their constituent sentences, in the second case not.

Apocalyptic — Daniel and Revelation — raises in an acute form the problem of just how literally biblical writing was intended to be taken. My own view, for what it's worth, is that dates were intended to be taken literally but talk of beasts and lightning is poetic. Daniel is concerned to predict an end which will happen an exact specified number of days after recognizable events. Whereas, fairly clearly, Revelation's talk of horses and dragons is symbolic. The kind of 'end' or 'day of the Lord' which some prophets are predicting is often of a lesser kind than the end of the world.[14] The description of chaos in Jeremiah 4: 23–6 is simply a prophecy of the fall of Jerusalem — bad enough, but only a kind of 'end', not the 'end of the world'. On the other hand the final chapters of Revelation, though not necessarily some of the earlier ones, do predict the end of the world. But unfortunately the exact conventions for reading apocalyptic are very unclear to the modern scholar.

A crucial issue of understanding each of the books mentioned in the last two paragraphs concerns the statements of purported authorship contained in them. The 'Screwtape Letters' were not written by Screwtape, although in a sense they purport to be. Our assessment of any truth-value which they contain will have no tendency to rule them out as containing falsity when it is discovered that they were written by C.S. Lewis. What of Ruth, and Daniel? Here again we simply do not know what were the local conventions. My guess is that authorship is irrelevant to 2 Esdras, but important for Daniel. Local convention would hold that there was falsity in the book of Daniel if it was shown that it had nothing to do with Daniel; that it did not derive from anyone influenced by him but was written three hundred years later than it claims to have been written. With the prophets, I suspect, it matters that something of what the book of Isaiah contains has been inspired by Isaiah, but it was quite acceptable to tack on oracles regarded as continuing Isaiah's teaching. And similarly for letters. So long as a letter contains some of St Paul's teaching, it was compatible with claiming Pauline origin for it that it develop Pauline teaching. The attribution of all law in Israel to Moses, all psalms to David, and all philosophical reflection ('wisdom literature') to Solomon was clearly recognized by some as not to be taken literally. (I Sam. 30:25 reports the promulgation by David of a new law.[15]) The point being made by this attribution is that law began with Moses, and later law developed his; and similarly for psalms and wisdom literature. The point was of course thoroughly misunderstood later, to the extent of supposing that Moses wrote the description of his own funeral. (See the last chapter of Deuteronomy, the 'fifth book of Moses'.)

It is for scholars to explain to us how to interpret the books in the light of the conventions of the time they were written, to analyse their truth-conditions. Those conditions are very far from clear, yet crucial for understanding the works.

III

So much for the truth-conditions of individual books of the Bible, considered on their own. In analysing these, I made a crucial assumption that the authors of these books were the ordinary human individuals or groups who compiled the books. But there is a different way of looking at the Bible. The books of the Bible were gradually put together as Scripture, as a whole work, which was eventually, later still, put together in one book — the Bible. The process was a gradual one — first of the Law, then of the prophets, then of the whole Old Testament; then by the Christian Church of parts of the New Testament, and then of the whole New Testament as a part of the whole Bible. Putting the books together into a whole Bible involved giving a change of context, and in consequence, by processes similar to those involved in the formation of an individual book, a change of meaning.

A crucial aspect of social context for the meaning of any sentence or book is who is its author and for whom it was written. For it is his social context and the cultural presuppositions of the author and his audience which dictate how the book is to be interpreted. The Church put the Bible together, but it did so by selecting books deriving from prophets or apostles in which were recorded what in its view was God's revelation through them to man. God, in the Church's view, was the ultimate author of the Bible — working, no doubt, through human writers with their own idiosyncracies of style, but all the same inspiring the individual books and inspiring the Church to recognize books of the right kind.

The view of God as the 'ultimate author' of the Bible divides, of course, into various views, from one which sees his contribution as the sole author dictating the sentences to the human 'authors' and the selection of books to the canonizers, through one which sees him as co-author along with the human authors and co-selector along with the canonizers, to one which sees him merely as providing background inspiration which sometimes was and sometimes was not followed.[16] However, in order to explore the consequences of a simple position, I shall work, to begin with, with the strong view that God was the author of the Bible in the strongest sense that he 'dictated' it.

I shall then comment on the consequences of modifying that view. We shall see that the view would have to be modified a great deal before it made any significant difference to the way in which the text is to be interpreted.

Now maybe God is not the author of the Bible in the strong (or any other) sense. And one consideration relevant to settling this matter is whether what is said in the Bible is true. For plausibly God will not lie to men on central matters of doctrine. But, I repeat, that is not a simple test, for what a text means depends on who wrote it. For example, as we saw earlier, it is the cultural presuppositions of its author and his audience which determine which sentences are to be taken metaphorically and which literally. And that brings us to the question of for whom was the Bible written. In the end for the whole world, no doubt. But which group was its most immediate audience, best able to understand its allusions and see the point of its stories? If God was its author, he would presumably ensure that the intended audience was the actual audience. Those who immediately received the Bible would be those for whom it was immediately intended. Hence the audience was the Church to which the Bible came and through which its message was proclaimed. But not, presumably, the Church of the fourth century AD alone, which finally assembled it, but the Church of earlier centuries as well, which used most of its books. And the process of refining biblical texts and of enquiring whether the books of the Apocrypha belong to the Bible never having stopped, there is point in saying that the process of canonization has never quite stopped. Further, in some ways which I shall examine shortly, the fourth-century Church held and, as we shall see, had to hold, that the Church of later centuries would sometimes be better able to interpret its message than it was itself. So the answer which I suggest is that, if God is the Bible's author, the Bible's audience was the Church of all centuries, including our own and yet future centuries.

So the question to ask about the Bible is whether what it says is true if it is interpreted under the supposition that God is its author and that the Church of past and future is its audience. We shall see shortly that, although that test can be applied, the truth or falsity of the Bible depends on the truth or falsity of the Creeds and central Christian doctrines, and cannot be

ascertained independently of those. Fortunately, content is not
the only test of authorship. There is another test in whether
God independently (e.g., through the Resurrection of Christ[17])
gave the Church some guarantee that its basic message would
be his. That test also does not give totally certain results; but
any evidence of an independent guarantee of the Church's
authority provides some guarantee as to who was the author of
the Bible and who was its intended audience.

So I proceed to investigate the question of the tests for what
the Bible does mean if God is its author in the strong sense and
the Church of many centuries is its intended audience. This
social and cultural context provides a framework making
possible disambiguation of what, as it stands, is a very ambiguous text. As it stands, it is a collection of separate books,
each having its own unity. There are no connecting verses
between the separate books nor any preface which explains the
relation of one book to another. There are many obvious inner
conflicts — for example, between Israelite leaders (apparently
on God's behalf) commending some pretty simple and rough
justice in the early books of the Bible, such as the book of
Judges; and Jesus (apparently on God's behalf) commending
non-violence in the Gospels. Is the Old Testament with its
ritual law and (in parts) rough justice, of equal authority with
the New? Or is the Old Testament simply the record of man
seeing some partial truth, more fully revealed in the New? Or,
alternatively, is the New the record of man losing a vision
grasped by the Old Testament? The slogan of Protestant con-
fessions, 'The infallible rule of interpretation of Scripture is the
Scripture itself,[18]' is quite hopeless. The Bible does not belong
to an obvious genre which provides rules for how overall
meaning is a function of meaning of individual books. We must
have a preface. And if not a preface in the same volume, a short
guide by the same author issued in the same way as the Bible,
providing disambiguation and publicly seen by the intended
audience to do so. Such a guide would be an extension of the
original work. And that said, there is of course such a guide. It
is the Church's Creeds and other tradition of public teaching of
items treated as central to the Gospel message. If the Church's
imprimatur shows in any way that God is the author of Scripture, it shows *a fortiori* that God is the author of its most central

teaching and above all the Creeds, which are shorter and easier documents to understand, allegiance to which was regarded as far more important at a far earlier stage of the Church's history than acknowledgment of the authority of Scripture. The Bible as promulgated by the Church must therefore be interpreted in the light of the Church's central teaching as a Christian document. That point was well taken early in the Church's history. 'Every word' of Scripture 'shall seem consistent' to someone, wrote Irenaeus, 'if he for his part diligently read the Scriptures, in company with those who are presbyters in the church, among whom is the apostolic doctrine.'[19]

The Creeds constrain the interpretation of the Bible, not vice versa. (Of course, the ground for affirming some of the statements in the Creeds is passages of the Bible. But for this purpose these passages are simply regarded as historical records, and do not have authority deriving from their place in the Bible.) Theology from without always dictated which sentences of the Bible were bench-marks by which other sentences were to be interpreted.[20] The consequence of this rule was, in view of what Christian teaching said about revelation given in Christ, that in any apparent clash between Old and New Testaments, the New took priority. Passages in the Old Testament in apparent conflict with the New were to be interpreted either as God's temporary and limited revelation superceded by the fuller revelation, or were to be interpreted metaphorically.

I now illustrate this point by a more detailed example. The Pentateuch, the first five books of the Old Testament, contains many detailed laws about justice and sacrifice, said to have been dictated by God himself. The Christian Church taught that much of this was no longer binding. So how were these laws to be taken now; why include them at all in the Bible? Christian apologetic of the early centuries, which led, against Marcion, to the inclusion of the Old Testament in a canon of Scripture, made one or other of two claims, both of which are to be found in Irenaeus, the principal champion of Old Testament canonicity in the days when it was at issue.

The first approach represents the law as a minimum standard of behaviour, consisting in detailed rules and backed up by precise punishments and rewards, useful for educating simple men, lacking in much natural love for God and their fellows. This approach takes its beginning from the words of Christ in St Matthew about divorce; Christ forbade divorce and in response to a question as to why Moses had allowed it stated that this was because of man's hardness of heart.[21] Irenaeus describes the rules of the Law as 'the laws of bondage',[22] suited for the instruction or punishment of the people, and cancelled now by the law of liberty. The ritual provisions of the Pentateuch, which might well be regarded as imperatives before, were now seen as firmly enclosed within quotation marks, reporting an original promulgation which the New Testament showed to be no longer binding.

The other and more prominent approach in Irenaeus is that the Law is to be allegorized. Sacrificial regulations were of importance because they symbolize by external gestures deeper future realities.[23] Although this particular approach to the ritual law derives its obvious Christian inspiration from the Epistle to the Hebrews, that ancient acts of importance are 'types' of future realities is a view deeply embedded in Hebrew and early Christian thought. Sometimes a prophet performs deliberately with symbolic gestures (e.g. Ezekiel 37: 15–28). Sometimes those who performed the ancient acts did so without considering any symbolic significance which they might have, but the Judaeo-Christian tradition expected to find in the Old Testament many 'types' of later developments, and, above all, of the events of the New Testament.

These two general approaches were available for resolving other clashes between Old and New Testaments. Any Old Testament doctrinal teaching, about exterminating the heathen for example, which, taken literally, clashed with New Testament teaching about turning the other cheek, could be reinterpreted as a simple message to primitive men, telling them the only way in which they could defend the purity of Israel — given their nomadic life and limited understanding of what such purity consisted in. It was binding on them but not on us, whose situation and range of possible understanding is different; to us the New Testament teaches (what Christian teaching generally affirms to be) an eternally binding message. The alternative is to read the Old Testament metaphorically — for example, God telling the Israelites to exterminate the Canaanites is God telling the Church to exterminate the seven

deadly sins, and so on. Both of these two methods were prac-
tised in the first millenium AD, though perhaps the second
predominated. Its practice was the utilization, in a culture
expecting to find allegories and types in religious documents in
a way in which we do not, of the techniques naturally and
readily available for interpreting passages which could not be
taken literally, of a kind with our own rules for recognizing
metaphor. The same method had been at work in the gradual
process by which the Jews had canonized the Old Testament.
The Song of Songs probably owed its incorporation into the
Jewish canon to the understanding that it was to be perceived
in a non-literal way.[24]

Our rules for recognizing metaphor clearly suggest that you
only take metaphorically a sentence which taken literally
would be obviously false or inappropriate in the context. Many
of the Fathers recognized that allegorizing could go too far. As
St Basil wrote: 'When I hear "grass", I understand by it grass,
and likewise with "plant", "fish", "beast" and "property", all
these words, in the sense in which they are spoken, thus I
understand them. For I am not ashamed of the Gospel.'[25] This,
however, clashes with a tradition developing in patristic times
but strong in the Middle Ages, that all passages have one or
more than one metaphorical sense. The general public rules for
recognizing metaphor do not, however, force any metaphorical
meaning on passages which can be taken literally, and the
Fathers who resisted excessive allegorizing recognized that, for
meaning is something determined by public criteria and once
you interpret metaphorically when public considerations do
not force you to, 'anything goes'.

But when the passage is to be taken metaphorically, what are
the rules for how it is to be taken? For metaphor in all contexts,
as we saw earlier, the rules are: take the words of the passage
(apart from words which link it to its context) in their literal
senses. Consider the objects or properties normally designated
by these words, and objects or properties commonly associated
with them. Interpret the words as designating the latter objects
or properties instead. Take literally the linking words. Take as
the true interpretation that which interprets the words as designating objects or properties closely rather than remotely connected with their normal designata, in so far as can be done in

a way which makes the sentence appropriate to the context. In so far as there is not one obvious such interpretation, the passage will be ambiguous. As the history of biblical interpretation suggests, these rules do yield the result that many biblical passages are ambiguous — but perhaps not as ambiguous as that history suggests. For the interpreter should take for first consideration objects or properties *closely* connected with those normally designated by the words at stake. And so interpretations which are not too far distant from the literal are to be preferred to more remote ones.

I have previously represented the 'historical' and 'metaphorical' ways of taking passages which could not be taken as literally true as two different ways. But the considerations of the last few paragraphs allow us to see them as much more closely connected. You take literally, if you can, statements of what was done and said at moments of history. If you cannot take these literally, only a metaphorical interpretation is open. If it is said or implied that God was the inspirer or author of certain actions or words, take that literally, if you can; otherwise take it metaphorically. If what God is said to have inspired or said clashes with the kind of character we know him to have on other grounds or with the kind of conduct he has commended elsewhere or conflicts with what we know otherwise to be true, then suppose that he limited his message or inspiration to what his original audience could understand. Or you can suppose that what he did was not what he is said to have done but the nearest thing to it which primitive Israel who originally first heard this message could understand. That is, he inspired men to do actions which, although not the best open to them, were the best which they could (with their limited understanding) see reason for doing; he said not what was true, but among the sentences which they could understand and see reason for believing, what was nearest to the truth. This is the 'historical' interpretation. But it inevitably suggests a deeper truth which could not be told to primitive Israel; and this we can get at by taking the passage metaphorically, not in a far-fetched allegorical way but simply by 'up-dating' the passage, considering what (in the light of the Christian Gospel and other evident truth) its message and inspiration would amount to if addressed to more sophisticated people in different situations. So the historical interpretation inevitably suggests a metaphorical one, but not a farfetched, detailed allegory. This point will be illustrated by a different kind of example from my earlier one. The truth obvious to the later Church with which literal interpretation may clash and which (given that it is part of a Book addressed to that later Church) forces reinterpretation, may be a scientific or historical truth, as well as a doctrinal truth. Take Genesis 1. Suppose we treat it not as a hymn, but wrongly (I suspect) as a document intended to be true sentence-by-sentence (i.e., whose total truth depends on the truth of each of its constituent sentences). Then, science suggests to us and suggested to the Church of the fourth century AD, it cannot be taken as literally true. Augustine thought this, though our reasons were not all his. He taught (in his commentary *De Genesi ad Litteram*) that the 'days' of creation could not be taken literally, because (in his view) there could only be 'days' when there was a Sun and the narrative recorded the creation of the Sun on only the fourth day. He was also worried about whether there really were in a literal sense 'waters above the firmament' (Gen. 1:7) on the grounds that any water in such parts far distant from the Sun and warm Earth would be frozen stiff. Although he produces scientific reasons for doubting the scientific argument, he does allow that it might work and so lead to the conclusion that the passage was to be taken metaphorically. Our (somewhat different) reasons for denying the literal truth of this passage need no spelling out by me. However, the interpretation nearest to the literal under which it comes out as plausibly true is derived by treating the 'days' as long periods of time and the detailed order of creation as not to be taken as too important. Then the passage tells us that gradually God brought about the various facets of creation over long periods of time (no doubt through secondary causes, as Gen. 2 suggests). This interpretation is what you get if you take the historical interpretation and then ask what is the point of its incorporation into Scripture.

Augustine also took the passage metaphorically, but his interpretation is by comparison a very far-fetched one. He claimed that all things described in Genesis 1 were created simultaneously, and that talk about 'days' is to be interpreted as talk about stages in the knowledge of creation possessed by the angels. My interpretation is much nearer to the text than Augustine's. For 'days' are more like billenia than they are like logical stages in the growth of knowledge. My metaphorical interpretation is, therefore, by normal criteria for metaphorical interpretation, better than his. Further, it does justice to the historical context to which it was originally addressed (be it by Moses, or some fifth-century hymn writer). It shows the point of its original utterance (which on more far-fetched interpretations it would not have) to convey, within the beliefs of the culture, the message of the dependence of 'all things visible and invisible' on the Creator. So the most plausible metaphorical interpretation is often that which fits with the historical interpretation, in helping us to see why God said what he did to the primitive Israel.

Aquinas made just these points, in connection with just the same text about 'waters above the firmament' which worried Augustine. If a theory can be 'seen to be false by solid arguments', it must not be regarded as the teaching of a Scriptural passage. 'Take into account rather, that Moses was speaking to ignorant people and out of condescension to their simpleness presented to them only those things immediately obvious to the senses.'[26]

Another and different kind of example concerns those Old Testament passages which seem to represent God as subject to emotion or as embodied. Christian doctrine taught that God was not like this. Hence passages which talk of God as 'angry' or 'striking' people down are not to be taken literally. They are to be taken as attributing to God properties as near as possible (in view of the context and God's known attributes) to those normally designated by these terms. If God is said to be 'angry', this 'anger' does not involve sensations in the stomach or an urge to cause hurt beyond what is just, but only a determination to do what is good in righting wrong justly. But the passages in which God is said to be angry occur in documents written by and for an unsophisticated people, inadequately aware of God's true nature. That is why the message of his determination to right wrong was put in terms of his anger. This point was common currency of the Fathers. Old Testament documents containing false theological doctrines were seen as promulgated by the Church, freed from those doctrines. Thus Novatian:

> The prophet was speaking about God at that point in symbolic language, fitted to that stage of belief, not as God was, but as the people were able to understand . . . God, therefore is not finite, but the people's understanding is finite; God is not limited, but the intellectual capacity of the people's mind is limited.[27]

If God is the author of Scripture, and also the author of the central claims of Christian doctrine embodied in the Creed, then, we have seen, the latter constrain the interpretation of the former. But truth evident to the speaker and his audience which shows some sentence taken literally to be false also forces a metaphorical interpretation on the sentence, whether that evident truth is contained in some other work of the same author or not. We have seen how Augustine and Aquinas both allowed that scientific discovery forced metaphorical interpretation on a text; for it was scientific 'discovery' which suggested that in a literal sense there were not 'waters beyond the firmament'. And Augustine belonged to the century which promulgated a canonized scripture. But if the intended audience of Scripture is the Church, not only of the first century (many of whom, presumably, Augustine would have regarded as scientifically backward) or the first four centuries, but of later centuries and millenia, truth evident to the latter must also be allowed to force a reinterpretation on the text in the way that truth evident to Augustine forced that. New scientific and historical discoveries may force that kind of reinterpretation. Now we know that the world began a lot longer ago than 4000 BC, and Methuselah did not really live to 969 years. So we take these passages in the sense nearest to the literal in which they come out as consistent with other evident truth and the credal framework which constrains all interpretations.

That the sense of some passages can be seen only in a 'future context' follows from my earlier point that if a social context is known only to a speaker and not his audience, they may not understand the meaning of a passage until they become familiar with that context. Scientific understanding may reveal the meaning of a passage; and so may new historical under-

standing, both of past and future. Predictions (and we have
seen that not all prophecies are predictions) may be understood
only when the time comes about which the prediction was
made. God could foresee the 'future context' of his prediction
in advance, and express his prediction in terms of that context,
whose meaning would only become clear to those without
foreknowledge when the time arrived. Biblical writers were not
unaware that he to whom a prediction was given could not
always understand it.[28] And some of the Fathers taught about
predictions, as I have done, that their meaning and truth would
become evident at the same time. That is, our understanding
some oracle and seeing its fulfilment will be simultaneous; when
we see certain things to be so, we will also see that that was what
the mysterious passage was getting at. Irenaeus writes 'every
prophecy is to men [full of] enigmas and ambiguities. But when
the time has arrived, and the prediction has come to pass, then
the prophecies have a clear and certain exposition.'[29]

The tradition of reinterpretation of biblical prophecy in the
light of history is itself a biblical tradition. Daniel 9 reinterprets
Jeremiah's talk of 'seventy years' (Jer. 25:12) as seventy 'weeks
of years'; and 2 Esdras 12:11 reinterprets Daniel 7:7. Those in
that tradition would not have been unduly disconcerted to
discover that in its original context the Book of Daniel proph-
esied an 'end' in the second century BC. They would have
reflected that the meaning of the prophecy was something other
than the human author's original understanding of it; and that
time would show what that meaning was. Perhaps the literal
'failure' of the prophecy makes clear that all prophecy is
warning, not prediction; and maybe that warning was heeded
by someone.

The conventions of literary genre peculiar to interpreting a
certain kind of text (e.g. a prophecy or a parable) must be ones
familiar to the intended audience — although they may
misapply them in a particular case (e.g., through ignorance of
scientific truth). What if the Church of different centuries
adopts different conventions of interpretation? In this matter
(which is a matter of literary convention, not scientific truth
independent of convention), by and large priority must go to
the Church of earlier centuries. For the Church of later centuries has before it the record of interpretation by the Church

of earlier centuries, but not vice-versa. Conventions of interpretation (e.g., whether you take a story such as Jonah as a
piece of history or a parable) make a difference as to how a
message is to be understood. The Bible's message cannot have
been meant by God to be hidden largely from earlier centuries.
They have only their conventions to go on; the later Church
can use the record of earlier interpretation.

The account which I have now given of how Scripture is to
be interpreted if God is supposed to be its author and the
Church of future centuries its intended audience, follows from
the general rules for interpreting texts which I have earlier
outlined. Investigate who is the author, who the intended
audience, what is the genre and what are the conventions for
interpreting works of that genre, interpret a work in terms of a
preface or other guide, take as metaphorical what the author
cannot have intended as literal, and so on: these are all very
general rules for understanding works and are in no way
peculiar to the Bible. It is just that they give results far from
obvious to modern men when applied to this case. Treating the
Bible 'like any other book' in the way you interpret it has the
consequence that it turns out to be very unlike any other book
in its pattern and structure.

This way of interpreting does not have the consequence that
nothing in the Bible can turn out to be false. For there are limits
to metaphorical interpretation, set by the understanding in my
way of treating it that the Bible was intended for the guidance
of the Church in the early centuries as well as the later centuries
AD. Hence, although it might contain some passage whose true
meaning would be apparent only to later centuries, it could not
contain passages which, interpreted in the light of the Creeds
and other central Christian doctrine, and with the presuppositions of those centuries, were importantly false. And what
would determine whether the falsity was important? If it was
important in a respect treated by the Creeds and other central
Christian doctrines as important. It follows from that that the
Bible can be shown false only in so far as the Creeds and central
doctrines can be shown false; for they constrain its interpretation. If it were shown false in this way, it would of course follow
that God was not its author in the strong sense with which I
have so far been concerned.

IV

There are, however, positions about biblical unity and authorship intermediate between those considered in sections II and
III. Section II treated the Bible as a collection of books with
human authors. Section III treated the Bible as one book with
God as its author in a strong sense. One may reasonably
suppose that in so far as the authority of the Church declared
God to be the author of the Bible, it declared him author in a
less direct way and that is what internal evidence also suggests.
It may be held that God is the author of the Bible only in the
sense that he inspired the human authors to write their books
and the canonizers to include in the Bible the books they did.
Not merely did those human authors have their own style and
presuppositions and God sought only to breathe his message
through those (as the strong interpretation allowed), but also
the human authors and canonizers were less than fully pliable.
They were not fully open to divine truth, and allowed some
small amount of falsity on important matters to infect Scripture. The Bible is like a symphony written and conducted by a
genius, but played by an orchestra of wilful amateurs.

But that is not going to make any significant difference to the
way in which the text is going to be interpreted — so long as
basically God is the inspirer and guide of Scripture. For how
are we to recognize the aberrations which human authors have
introduced into the biblical message? In the same way as one
would recognize errors of transmission in any other work of art
or literature — by their discrepancy with the main message.
Hence we do not take as literal truth anything at odds with the
central message of the Bible; and that, if God is its author, is,
by previous arguments, the message of the Church's creeds.
But, by the arguments of the last section, we do not take such
passages as literally true anyway, even if God is the 'dictator'
of every word of the Bible. The only difference is that if God is
the dictator, we regard all passages at odds with the Bible's
central message as having metaphorical truth; whereas if he is
only an 'inspirer' whose inspiration may not always be
followed, we must regard some such passages as false, since they
have been written contrary to his inspiration and so have
human authors as their authors and so different criteria of

meaning, which may often pick them out as having a literal meaning as their intended meaning. But there will be no way of distinguishing among those passages which are literally false, those which are just false and those which have metaphorical truth. If God is regarded as sufficiently the inspirer of the Bible to influence to a very large degree which books were canonized, then most literally false passages will be metaphorically true. And, since we can never give a passage a meaning at odds with the Bible's main message or with evident truth, we can come to little harm in supposing all literally false passages to have such metaphorical sense as to make them true.

Suppose some writer, say the author of Psalm 137, allows some excessively vengeful sentiment to enter the text, contrary to his better judgement (e.g., in verse 9 declaring of the Babylon which took the Israelites into captivity 'Blessed shall he be that taketh thy children; and throweth them against the stones'). The basic New Testament teaching, 'bless them that persecute you, bless and curse not' (Romans 12:14) forces this text to be understood in the light of it either as a human insertion or metaphorically, for example, Babylon as Satan and his 'children' as the sins which he attempts to graft on to men. Taking seriously the notion of God as the inspirer, via authors and canonizers, of the whole text forces a consistent interpretation on the text — just as inserting a few verses at the end of Ecclesiastes forces upon the text of the earlier chapters a meaning which they would lack without it. It is only if one came to have so weak a doctrine of biblical inspiration that one regarded the books of the Bible as basically of human origin — for example Psalm 137 as on its own written by a psalmist on his own initiative — that it can be seen as in conflict with basic Christian doctrines.

The view that biblical passages are to be interpreted in the light of those doctrines does not have the consequence that they have no more content than those doctrines. On the contrary they illustrate them abundantly. Interpreted in this way, they show God gradually getting his message across to Israel through the way in which he dealt with Israel over many centuries; culminating in all the details of divine action and propositional revelation through Jesus Christ. But why, then, a Bible with such complicated rules of interpretation? Why not a

500-page Creed (viz., a Denzinger)? Because it matters that
God allowed men to grasp those doctrines through an interaction with him in the context of human history, and sacred
scripture will record how that came about. Because it matters
that those doctrines are expressible in the presuppositions of
cultures which are scientifically and historically ignorant.
Because it matters too that men shall continue to struggle to
understand their faith more deeply; and wrestling with the
biblical text with the help of others who have done the same
under the guidance of basic Christian doctrine is a profound
way of doing this. And because such a complicated way of
expressing the doctrines reminds us, what a 500-page creed
would hide from us, that divine truth is often far too profound
to be captured adequately by any human sentences.

The way of understanding the Bible which I have derived
from basic philosophical principles about meaning was that of
so many of the Fathers who canonized the biblical books. It was
made explicit by Origen (*De Principiis* 4.3) (though in practice
Origen allegorized much more than his principles warranted,
and that made others of the Fathers suspicious of Origen's
treatment of Scripture). The Church Fathers read the Scriptural books in this way and they would not have given them
canonical status if they had not done so. The context of the
canon and its promulgation meant that some passages were to
be understood as containing limited and partial truth and some
passages were to be understood metaphorically. It was the book
understood in that way they declared to be true. And, by and
large, with many qualifications, that was the way of understanding the Bible common in the Church, common even to
Catholics and Protestants, until the nineteenth century, when
the Bible came to be interpreted by many Anglo-Saxon Protestants in perhaps the most literal and insensitive way in which
it has ever been interpreted in Christian history. This literalism
was encouraged by the basic philosophical mistake of equating
the 'original meaning' of the text, gradually being probed by
historical enquiry, with the meaning of the text in the context
of a Christian document. We may hanker after the 'original
meaning' in the sense of the meaning of the separate units
before they were used to form a Bible, but that sense is *not*
relevant to assessing its truth. We may not like treating the

Song of Songs allegorically, preferring its 'literal' sense; but its literal sense was not the sense in which those who gave it canonical status understood it. If we wish to take seriously claims for the truth of the Bible, we must understand it in the way that both philosophical rules for interpreting other texts and the original canonizers suggest, and that includes their admission that it contained deeper truths which future generations wiser than themselves might detect by using their rules. The genetic fallacy that origins determine present operation leads us to suppose that we understand the meaning of a text when we understand its literary history. But we do not; what we need to know is its literary context, not its literary history.

1 Where the sentence is embedded in a large repeatable context, as a sentence of a book of which there may be many copies or of a play of which there may be many performances, I count all tokens of the sentence in that context as the same token, as long as the context remains qualitatively identical in all respects which affect the meaning of the token utterance, e.g., so long as the sentence remains part of the play and is not used for some other purpose.

2 For further elaboration of this point, see my paper 'Analogy and Metaphor', in G.J. Hughes (ed.) *The Philosophical Assessment of Theology*, essays in Honour of Frederick C. Coplestone, Search Press, 1987.

3 'On Denoting', reprinted in (ed. Robert C. Marsh) Bertrand Russell, *Logic and Knowledge*, London, 1956.

4 'On Referring' in P.F. Strawson, *Logico-Linguistic Papers*, Methuen & Co., 1971.

5 This view is associated with Donnellan (Keith S. Donnellan, 'Reference and Definite Descriptions', *Philosophical Review* 1966, 75, 281–304; and 'Speaker Reference, Descriptions, and Anaphora' in (ed.) P.A. French et al., *Contemporary Perspectives in the Philosophy of Language*, University of Minnesota Press, 1979). However, what Donnellan actually claims is that, so long as by the description 'the man drinking martini' I was intending my hearers to pick out a certain man, then the man to whom I refer is the man to whom I am intending to refer. My intention suffices, whatever the indications or lack of them provided by the context, to secure reference. At least this is so, claims Donnellan, of definite descriptions used referentially. Donnellan distinguishes the attributive from the referring use of definite descriptions. 'The A' used attributively in 'The A is B' says merely 'Whoever is the A is B'; 'the A' used referentially is simply a device for picking out an object which could be picked out in other ways; the fact that the description 'the A' applies to it is not of importance for what is

being said. Donnellan's cited claim concerns only definite descriptions used referentially. However, it must only hold when the context makes clear to whom the speaker was intending to refer; for meaning is a public matter and a mere intention to refer to some individual cannot ensure that the speaker does so refer. For if Donnellan was right one could never say in such cases 'Even if what you meant to say was true, what you actually said was false'; and that surely is a comment which must always have application to all public assertions. Unless the context does make clear that the intended reference (speaker's reference) is other than the object picked out by the description (semantic reference), then the reference is the semantic reference. This account must be extended to proper names, as when I say 'John looks tired' but the context reveals that I mean that George looks tired (as Kripke pointed out (see S.A. Kripke, 'Speaker's Reference and Semantic Reference' in (ed.) P.A. French et al., *Contemporary Perspectives in the Philosophy of Language*, University of Minnesota Press, 1979.)

For full-length discussion of the criteria for determining to which (if any) object a referring expression refers, see Gareth Evans, *The Varieties of Reference*, Oxford, 1982, especially Chapter 9.

6 See S.A. Kripke, op. cit., on this.

7 This argument is often implicit in some passage rather than explicit. One place where it is fairly near to the surface is pp.272–82 of H. Putnam, 'Language and Reality', in his *Mind, Language and Reality*, Philosophical Papers, Vol.2, Cambridge University Press, 1975.

8 For a full discussion of some of the tests which can be used to detect when a biblical fragment is being used metaphorically, see G.B. Caird, *The Language and Imagery of the Bible*, Duckworth 1980, Chapter 11.

9 On the extent to which this is the correct way of interpreting a parable, see Caird, op. cit., ch. 9. See p.166 for his comment on the parable of the sower.

10 See Ezekiel 33.14f. for explicit affirmation that prophecies of doom were to be so interpreted. See also the whole story of Jonah.

11 See B.S. Childs, *Introduction to the Old Testament as Scripture*, SCM Press, 2nd edition 1983, p. 150. See also J. Barton, *Reading the Old Testament*, Darton, Longman and Todd, 1984, pp. 50f.

12 See the discussion of this and other examples in Caird, op. cit., pp. 184ff. and pp. 213ff.

13 Perhaps the most openly fictional work is the Book of Judith. See the discussion in Caird, op. cit., p. 206.

14 See the discussion of this in Caird, op. cit., pp. 256–60.

15 See Caird, op. cit., pp. 205f.

16 On different ways of understanding the 'inspiration' of the Bible, and defence of a preferred such way, see W.J. Abraham, *The Divine Inspiration of Holy Scripture*, Oxford University Press, 1981.

17 For argument on how Christ's resurrection would be evidence of the truth of his teaching, see my *Faith and Reason*, Clarendon Press, 1981, pp. 189–93.

18 See (e.g.) Article 1 of the Westminster Confession.
19 *Adversus Haereses*, 4.32.1.
20 This is one of the themes of James Barr, *Holy Scripture: Canon, Authority, Criticism*, Clarendon Press, 1983. See, for example, pp. 39ff.
21 Matthew 19:7f., commented on by Irenaeus in *Adversus Haereses* 4.15.2.
22 *Adversus Haereses* 4.16.5.
23 *Ibid.*, 4.32.2.
24 'The Song of Songs owed its final acceptance to allegorical interpretation' — G.W. Anderson, 'The Old Testament: Canonical and Non-Canonical' in (ed.) P.R. Ackroyd and C.F. Evans, *The Cambridge History of the Bible*, Vol.I, Cambridge University Press, 1979, p. 134.
25 St Basil, *In Hexaemeron*, 188.
26 *Summa Theologiae*, Ia. 68.3 (Volume 10 of Blackfriars edition, translated by William Wallace OP, Blackfriars 1967).
27 Novatian, *De Trinitate* 6. Quoted in *Cambridge History of the Bible*, Vol.I, p. 451f. For this and other reasons for taking biblical passages metaphorically see B. Pascal, *Pensées* (Translated A.J. Krailsheimer), Penguin 1966, No. 272 and No. 501.
28 The purported author of the Book of Daniel claimed not to understand his prophecies — 'I heard, but I understood not', Dan. 12:8.
29 Irenaeus, *Adversus Haereses* 4.26.

The Concept of Revelation

STEWART R. SUTHERLAND

I

THERE are two introductory comments which I wish to make, and which will serve to set out the backcloth against which the arguments of this chapter will be developed.

(1)   As with many terms which have their life and find their meaning within the context of religious belief, the words 're-velation' and 'revelatory' have uses within contexts other than religious. Thus one can describe remarks, or the actions of an individual, or events, as variously 'revealing' or 'revelatory', or even in some cases as 'revelations', and do so when these words, deeds or events belong quite clearly to the interchanges of social, political and day-to-day life. What these uses share with more clearly religious uses of these terms is the element of uncovering what was hidden, including perhaps a removal of barriers within the perceiver. One most important point of difference is that in the non-religious cases the revelation can be, and often is, perhaps a slip, or even a mistake. Freud, of course exploited this sense *ad absurdum*. In the religious cases however, revelation is never the result of inattention, or mistakes. God, so to speak, never lets the cat out of the bag, whereas Mr Reagan frequently does, and Mrs Thatcher and President Mitterand occasionally do.

However, having drawn such a distinction, it is tempting and would be mistaken to assume that there are two very different and unrelated senses of the terms 'revelation' and 'revelatory' — the religious and the non-religious. My argument on this point will have two elements. The first is that while quite

certainly there are cases where there are clear differences
between the religious and non-religious uses of these terms,
equally there are areas of overlap and interpenetration where
one would be hard put to draw sharp boundary lines. This, if
true, is an important feature of the concept of revelation. The
second element of my argument concerns the theological
presuppositions with which we are working, and will be best
elaborated under (2) below.

(2)   A crude but initially useful distinction can be drawn
between two different pictures within which the concept of
revelation may be given a role. Not surprisingly, different
pictures imply rather different logical contours for the notions
of 'revelation' and 'revelatory' happenings. The two pictures
correspond very roughly to two different tendencies in post-
Kantian theology. The presuppositions which can be seen in
each are not necessarily incompatible, but in different theological emphases one picture can easily dominate and exclude the
other. Their power to do this depends upon the extent to which
their status as imaginative representations is forgotten because
of their very simplicity and potential comprehensiveness.

Picture (a) is a two-level picture in which behind the empirical world of phenomena there lies a second world of ultimate or
spiritual reality. The content of revelation is then the nature of
this 'other' world, from knowledge of which we are barred
variously by our finitude, by the veil of perception, by the
conceptual structures of the Kantian categories, or by our
sinfulness or spiritual blindness. The idea of an initiative
(God's) from this other world is seen as central and the knowledge or insight given will clearly be of a different order from
such knowledge as we have of the phenomenal or empirical
world. This will quite certainly carry important implications
for the *process* of revelation and for our account of what
phenomena are revelatory. However, there are a number of
options here and the specific route taken will depend upon how
the picture is filled out imaginatively (in prayer, preaching and
ritual) and conceptually (in the process of theological and
philosophical reflection). Of course when these do not go hand
in hand problems arise.

Picture (b) is one in which the metaphor of 'depth' is central.
One is depicted as trying to perceive the structures or substruc-

tures of this world, rather than trying to understand this world better by gaining knowledge of another ultimate reality. Equally, however, there are barriers to our perception of what is real, but these barriers are barriers to a true understanding of the one world and one reality which there is. Clearly, secular versions of these pictures are plentiful, and fairly recently the metaphor of 'depth' has been all but reduced to exhaustion by over-use — 'depth psychology', 'depth grammar', 'depth (linguistic) structures' etc. However, there are many notable religious uses of this picture (and to some extent, this metaphor) in views ranging from pantheism, through pan-en-theism, to the theology of Paul Tillich. What is most significant about such a picture is that it poses a rather different set of questions for our account of the concept of revelation. Notably there is less pressure for an emphasis upon the initiative of a God who is revealing *another* world to which he belongs and from which we are metaphysically as well as cognitively separated.

These two pictures are almost caricatures, but they do represent opposite ends of a spectrum of views which inform much theological thought, and which provide the imaginative unity which most believers find necessary in worship, prayer and ritual, as well as in the formulation of beliefs. Despite the crudeness of the distinction, it is, I believe, valuable to remind ourselves of these differing emphases for they do have profound implications for our account of the concept of revelation. What they do both show quite starkly is that the concept of revelation cannot be considered apart from its theological surroundings. On the one hand the account which we give will reveal much about our theology, and on the other, difficulties in giving a clear account of what is meant by 'revelation' and 'revelatory', may well be symptomatic of, or even entailed by, underlying problems in theology.

II

Dictionary definitions of 'revelation' specify two different uses of the term: one is to denominate *what* is revealed or disclosed, and the other is to denominate the *process* of disclosure or revelation. This suggests a division of lines of enquiry which can be indicated by asking two different questions.

(i)   What is distinctive about what is revealed or disclosed, about the truths or revelation?

(ii)   What is distinctive about the process of revelation or disclosure?

In the end I believe that the answers to these two questions are interdependent, but that the difficulties involved in answering the former have led to an unhelpful preoccupation with the latter. Such a preoccupation is not surprising, for of course, if a central characteristic of revealed truths is that to many, if not the majority, and for most of the time, they are hidden, then it seems both wiser and more profitable to concentrate upon the phenomena of revelation. Inevitably the process of revelation must have a phenomenal or empirical aspect and in principle that must be publicly available and therefore, with whatever difficulty, at least in principle amenable to discussion.

Again, however, and this is part of the paradox of the idea of revelation, unless we have *some* idea of the sorts of truths which might be disclosed in revelation, how do we know which types of phenomena and processes are suitable candidates for being revelatory? Thus, for example, for Bultmann, the phenomena which are the public aspect of the *event* of revelation are as they very variously are because of the types of truth which are to be revealed. Equally the phenomena to which a Paley or a Butler turn in search of disclosure are identified by reference to a complicated view about the content of what is to be disclosed, and by a complex theology of the relation of the world to God.

My proposal then is that we should concentrate upon the question of what if anything can be said about the distinctiveness of the truths of revelation. However, before moving to that stage of the discussion, it would be well to underline the unsatisfactory character of a preoccupation with the process of revelation.

If one asks what is distinctive about the process of revelation or disclosure, then it seems to me that there are three different sorts of point which can be made by way of reply.

The first is an essentially negative point that the very essence of the idea of revelation is that one should arrive at truth by other than 'the usual channels'. This is quite compatible with the popular insistence that 'in principle everything can be a means for revelation', for the point is that of course if everything can in principle be a means of revelation, so everything can in

principle be a barrier to our distraction from what is 'ultimately' true. Why else would we need revelation? Revelation is
premissed upon there being barriers to certain truths or types
of truth. These barriers are impenetrable to our normal or
'natural' way of seeking truth. So far so good, but of course this
is a purely negative point which is no more and no less than a
confession of limitation. Different accounts of revelation give
differing emphases to this negative point — some restricting it
to standard uses of discursive reasoning (Aquinas, *Summa Theologiae* 1a Q.12 is an admirable example of a subtle and sophisticated version of such a view), and others insisting that all
human faculties have the limitations of fallen creatures
(contrast the early Barth with Brunner, and in very different
terms with Schleiermacher on this point). This negative claim
is important (in whatever form) but it does not take us very far.

The second sort of remark which is sometimes offered about
the distinctiveness of the process of disclosure or revelation,
points us away from the phenomena by insisting (quite
properly within this view) that what is distinctive is non-
phenomenal, i.e. what is distinctive about the process is that
whatever phenomena may be used as *means*, ultimately one is
talking about an act or initiative from God (Kierkegaard and
Barth) or of a supernatural agency. Farrer offers a clear statement of what the latter amounts to in *The Glass of Vision*:

> Not that, if God acts supernaturally, he acts without second
> causes; but he works through second causes effects which do not
> arise from the natural powers of those causes.[1]

My reservation about pursuing these proposals as fruitful lines
of enquiry as they stand, is that they will not answer the
question 'What phenomena are revelatory?' without appealing
either to the content of revelation (for how else would we know
which second causes have been used by God?) or by elaborating
in much greater detail (as Farrer does elsewhere and as the
early Barth refused to do) reasons for suggesting why we might
expect God might use *these* rather than *those* second causes.
Again such an elaboration may only proceed on the basis of
some prior understanding of the *content* of revelation. Thus once
more we are referred back to our first question about the
distinctiveness of the contents or truths of revelation.

The third, and for our purposes final, focus of discussion

about the process of revelation is upon the concept of authority. It follows from the first negative point made that if the 'usual channels' of enquiry are not adequate, then alternative channels must be found. This often leads to preoccupation with the idea of certain sources of belief carrying the authority of sanctification and/or privileged access to the ultimate source of all truth. The authority has been variously an individual or group, a set of writings, or, more particularly as Picture (b) predominates, an initiation or pattern of discipline.

The issues raised by such a proposal, or set of proposals, would require an additional paper. Suffice it to say that I do not think that one can separate questions about authoritative sources of revelation from questions about the truth of the content of revelation. If a religion requires that one should accept the truth of what certain sources proclaim irrespective of the content of those claims, then so much the worse for the form of religion. Such forms of religion do exist, but they are not definitive of what religion is and must be.

III

What is distinctive about the truths of revelation?

There are two rather different types of criteria which one might wish to apply here. The first set would look to 'external' characteristics of the truths in question. For example one might regard them as distinctive because of the type of context in which these truths were revealed or discovered. Some theologians have pressed this point by giving great significance to the sermon, or 'the event of proclamation'. Alternatively one might stress particular experiential factors. Consider however, one such example:

> While I was thus in the act of calling upon God, I discovered a light appearing in my room, which continued to increase until the room was lighter than at noonday, when immediately a personage appeared at my bedside, standing in the air, for his feet did not touch the floor.

> He had on a loose robe of most exquisite whiteness. It was a whiteness beyond anything earthly I had ever seen: nor do I believe that any earthly thing could be made to appear so

exceedingly white and brilliant. His hands were naked, and his arms also, a little about the wrists; so, also, were his feet naked, as were his legs, a little above the ankles. His head and neck were also bare. I could discover that he had no other clothing on but this robe, as it was open, so that I could see into his bosom . . .

He called me by name, and said unto me that he was a messenger sent from the presence of God to me, and that his name was Moroni; that God had work for me to do . . . He said there was a book deposited, written upon gold plate, giving an account of the former inhabitants of this continent, and the source from whence they sprang. He also said that the fulness of the everlasting Gospel was contained in it, as delivered by the Saviour to the ancient inhabitants.

(Joseph Smith, from the introduction to *The Book of Mormon*)

This description is typical of one form of revelatory experience and would on an unreflective basis be thought to carry many of the appropriate external characteristics of such revelations. However, the unfruitfulness of this as a line of enquiry, comparable to my rejection of focussing upon the *process* of revelation, can be seen from the fact that this particular example is taken from Joseph Smith's introduction to *The Book of Mormon*. Even Mormons would agree that *ipso facto* that would for many disqualify it as the description of a revelatory experience. *Mutatis mutandis* the same would apply to descriptions taken from the New Testament, the Koran, the *Divine Principle* etc. Once again we are driven back to the need to discuss the content or at least internal characteristics of revealed truths, though as we shall see there are some 'external' characteristics of revealed truths which are important, and non-controversial.

There are four characteristics of revealed truths all of which are definitive and each of which I wish to discuss briefly before concentrating upon the last:

(i) What is revealed is true.
(ii) What is revealed is hidden and must be uncovered.
(iii) What is revealed has been 'hidden' because there are barriers within men and women which prevented its assimilation and appropriation.
(iv) There is always 'news' in what is revealed.

Each of these requires some elucidation.

(i)   *What is revealed is true.* This is an analytic truth comparable to 'what is known is true'. If something is properly described as 'revealed', then it is true. This analytic connection if not fully understood can be a source of error and danger. If this claim were regarded as being synthetically true, then there would be danger. However, if this claim is, rather, analytically true, then in application it has the form of a conditional.

(i.a)   If X is revealed, X is true, (cf. If X is known, X is true). This form shows *both* that if something is revealed and recognized as such then it may not properly be doubted, *and* that if it is doubted, then *ipso facto* its status as revealed is under question. The latter amounts to the claim that if there are grounds for doubting the truth of a claim indicated as revealed, then there are grounds for doubting it is revealed. For some theologians that may prove to be unacceptable, but if the connection is analytic then these consequences do follow.

The comparison between 'revealed' and 'known' in this context is important, but one cucial difference must be noted. This is best brought out by appeal to the standard definition of knowledge as 'justified true belief'. In generally accepted accounts of what this means, the element of justification carries with it the notion of justification that is at least in principle public — it implies that if X claims justifiably to believe B and the extent of the justification is such that X knows B, then Y, if presented with the same range of evidence or the same justification would also be in a position to know B. Of course, in classic examples of alleged revelations there is no parallel. For example, there is no indication that Saul's companions on the road to Damascus had anything 'revealed' to them. The revelation was not in principle public, it was to Saul. This is a feature of many 'revelations' which will be explored further.

(ii)   *What is revealed is hidden and must be uncovered.* This point is reasonably straightforward, but it does have 'bite' as we shall see when the fourth characteristic is discussed. It is of course open to rather different interpretations — depending for example upon whether we emphasize Picture (a) or Picture (b). This characteristic of the revealed truths of religion is of course that which it most clearly shares with such truths from non-religious contexts as are candidates for the description 'revealed'. The crucial question which is raised by this characteristic concerns the manner and nature of the hiddennes of those truths which are to be revealed.

(iii) *What is revealed has been 'hidden' because there are barriers within men and women which prevent its assimilation and appropriation.* I have three short comments to make on these 'barriers'.

(iii.a) They are not simply the barriers of carelessness. Revealed truths are not truths which are overlooked, and which are therefore immediately apparent to more attentive members of the community.

(iii.b) Likewise the barriers are not merely cognitive. It is not a matter of luck or intellectual ability or cognitive skill.

(iii.c.) Theologically within the Christian tradition the barrier is referred to as 'sin'. The implication is that there is a resistance to the truths involved, and whether active or passive this resistance cannot be set aside or overcome by human effort alone. Kierkegaard, for example, stresses this point strongly, arguing in *Philosophical Fragments* that what is lacking is the capacity or condition of receiving ultimate truth. Such a lack can be met not by human resources, but by God alone. This essentially is the difference between Socrates and Jesus. Socrates was for some the *occasion* of learning. He was a teacher from whom, as it so happened, some learned important truths. Jesus, however, was the revealer without whom certain truths could not be learned, for he gave not simply truths, but the possibility of appropriating those truths. All this suggests that there must be something quite distinctive about the truths in question, which makes them subject to such barriers.

(iv) *There is always 'news' in what is revealed.* Since I have already by implication ruled out, under (iii.a) and (iii.b) above, the possibility that the 'news' which is to be revealed is simply a matter of information or facts which have so far eluded us, there must be some alternative account of what is new about the truths of revelation.

This will be offered in the final section of the paper.

IV

Within the context of religion, including the Christian religion, there have been two different sorts of truths which have been thought to belong particularly to the context of revelation. On the one hand truths about the nature of God, or what is ultimate, have been regarded as having and requiring revealed status, and on the other so also have truths not simply about the human but about *my* ultimate condition or state (e.g. that *I* am a sinner, or fallen, that *I* am called to special tasks etc.).

Although they can be distinguished, these types of truths are in principle interdependent, for I cannot believe myself to be a sinner, or fallen, or saved unless I believe certain things about God, or what is ultimate. Inevitably therefore, the place which we take on the spectrum between Picture (a) and Picture (b) will have far-reaching consequences for our account of the sense to be given to either form of 'news'.

In order to give flesh to the bones of these abstract points, let us consider the revelation which lies at the heart of Christianity — that Jesus is the Christ.

At once we find a prima facie puzzle, for often it is said that Jesus is the revealer or the revelation. However, this apparent worry need not detain us, for in the account which I shall propose, the difficulty disappears.

If the claim that the central revelation of Christianity is that Jesus is the Christ, then if this claim has content, it must imply, within all the conventions of the Judaism which gave birth to Christianity, that in Jesus something about God, or what is ultimate (or as I prefer to put it, about what is eternal) is revealed. To work out fully the implications of this would require a whole volume, but for our purposes, three points will suffice.

(a)   At the heart of the claim that Jesus is the Christ, that a man has embodied or manifested what is divine or eternal, lies the claim that such notions as 'God' or 'divinity' or 'the eternal' have content. In the first but not of course the only place, there is an affirmation that the notion of divinity is neither empty nor unintelligible. It has been made manifest; it has been revealed; it has content; it is neither beyond sense nor sensibility. That, if true, is news indeed.

(b)   Within such a revelation is contained the further affirmation of what the content of the idea is. Affirmations are being made, revelation is given of what God is like, of the nature of divinity and of the eternal. Clearly just what that content is has been much disputed within the history of Christianity, and I do not propose to enter that argument now.

However, that there is dispute, is itself significant, for it implies
on Picture (a) that revelation is either rather more muted than
one might expect, or is in fact selective. On Picture (b) the
converse point is to be seen perhaps in the metaphor of peering
into depths, dimly divining. This in turn suggests not so much
a muted revelation as a muted sense of revelation.

(c) A third very important point which arises out of our
consideration of this concrete example is that this 'revelation'
has a place within a developing tradition. Indeed there is a
sense in which it created what became a new tradition. But at
the heart of the 'news' involved is a delicate although at times
a brutal interplay between the old and the new. The 'news' was
in part the correction and extension of what had been believed
about God and eternity. Its form was in part dictated by what
it was correcting and extending, and in part by the content of
what was new.

Uncharacteristically perhaps for a philosopher, I wish to
conclude my paper by focusing attention on a passage from the
Christian Scriptures whose explication would, I believe, exem-
plify all the points which I have been making in this paper. The
passage is one of the Synoptic Gospel accounts of the crucifixion
of Jesus, and particularly the two verses in that account (from
Matthew) which themselves build layer upon layer of the
metaphor or revelation by allusion to the rending of the veil of the
temple. That revealing, that unveiling, is part of the content of
the manifestation of the divine and eternal in the crucifixion of
Jesus. To understand that is to begin to give content to the
claim that Jesus is the Christ — and further, to the central
Christian belief that *this* is the revelation of God.

> Jesus, when he had cried again with a loud voice, yielded up the
> ghost.
> And behold, the veil of the temple was rent in twain from the
> top to the bottom; and the earth did quake, and the rocks rent.
>
> (Mathew 27:50–51)

1. A.M. Farrer, *The Glass of Vision*, London, Dacre Press, 1948, p. 4.

Faith and Philosophy

FREDERICK C. COPLESTON

I N the nineteenth century, some Russian thinkers called for the development of philosophical thought in harmony with (or, better, within the area or framework of) Christian faith. This call was expressed by the Slavophile writers Ivan Kireevsky (1806–56) and Aleksey Khomyakov (1804–60), and a sustained attempt to answer it was made by the eminent religious philosopher Vladimir Solovyev (1853–1900). As for the religiously oriented Russian thinkers who were expelled from their homeland in 1922, in spite of the very considerable differences between their philosophical ideas, writers such as Semyon Frank (1877–1950), Nikolai Berdyaev (1874–1948) and N.O. Lossky (1870–1965) were at one in hoping that their philosophical reflection would contribute to the enrichment of the Christian vision of the world and of human life and history.

Obviously, the demand for the development of philosophy in close union with or within the area of faith can be largely accounted for in terms of the relevant cultural context. As Kireevsky and Khomyakov saw the situation, philosophical thought in Western Europe, with some exceptions of course, had succumbed to a spirit of arid rationalism which, in its growth, had promoted indifference to or even contempt for religious faith. As Russia's increasing opening to the West had exposed the country to this line of thought, an antidote was needed. To look to the official representatives of Russian Orthodoxy for an effective remedy would be over-optimistic. What was required was a development of philosophical thought which would serve as a path to Christian faith.

As for Solovyev, he was faced by a radical intelligentsia which had been strongly influenced by Western positivism and materialism. Generally speaking, its members regarded religion as harmful superstition and the Russian Church as a lackey of the imperial regime. As a boy, Solovyev enthusiastically embraced atheism and adopted the attitude of the radical intelligentsia, until his atheist position was shaken by a study of Spinoza, whose thought contributed to the formation of Solovyev's theory of total-unity, the Absolute. From the age of eighteen Solovyev was a Christian believer, and he aspired to develop a philosophy which would not only be compatible with religious faith but which would also raise this faith to a new level of reflective consciousness, a level at which it could exercise a powerful transforming influence both on the individual's intellectual view of reality and on social and political life.

Though, however, it is easy enough to account, in terms of the cultural context, for the demand that philosophical thought should be developed in close union with Christian faith or that faith should be recognized as the basis for philosophical reflection, it is by no means so easy to decide precisely what such a demand implies. Needless to say, we cannot justifiably assume that all the Russian thinkers in question conceived the relation between faith and philosophy in the same way. Nor can we safely take it for granted that a given thinker must have formulated for himself a clear idea of the way in which the relation should be understood. But no comprehensive exegesis can be attempted here. I shall confine myself to discussing briefly certain selected lines of thought.

When Kireevsky attacked rationalism, he understood by this term the claim that the human understanding, regarded as grasping the logical connections between concepts, is the sole source and arbiter of truth. This claim, he insisted, was a one-sided exaggeration. The empiricists rightly attributed an important role in the attainment of truth to sense-experience. At the same time the truths required for living a full human life could be provided neither by reason alone nor by sense-experience alone nor even simply by both combined. What was needed was that the human being's psychical powers, including, for example, aesthetic intuition and what Pascal called 'the heart ', should operate in unified harmony. Given a recovery of 'mental wholeness', a philosophy could be developed, Kireevsky hoped, which would express 'integral knowledge' and constitute a path to religious faith rather than away from it.

Mention of philosophy as a path to faith may suggest the idea of an external instrument to be used in support of faith. The same sort of impression is likely to be conveyed by Solovyev's remark, if taken simply by itself, that philosophy's task is 'to justify the faith of our fathers'.[1] What Kireevsky came to desire, however, was a philosophy issuing from or stimulated by faith and remaining faithful to the spirit of Russian Orthodoxy. As for Solovyev, when he referred to philosophy as justifying the faith of 'our fathers', he was thinking, so he tells us, of faith being raised to the level of rational consciousness through philosophical reflection. He conceived religion as involving the vision of total-unity, of God in all and all in God, and he attributed to philosophy of religion the task of thinking through this idea of total-unity and exhibiting its truth. The kinds of philosophy which he had in mind would therefore presuppose faith and operate from within it, rather than act as a purely external buttress to Christian belief.

Solovyev was convinced, doubtless rightly, that a rebirth of vigorous intellectual life within the community of Orthodox believers was a crying need. He was also convinced that even the more learned among the official representatives of Russian Orthodoxy showed little ability to communicate effectively with those who had embraced non-religious or anti-religious outlooks. But, it may be urged, if philosophy is to fill the place of a living theology, if it is conceived as presupposing faith and as undertaking to raise faith's content to a new level of reflective consciousness, must not this process be seen as involving the transformation of naive faith into speculative metaphysics? When, in his youth, Solovyev turned from the study of Spinoza to that of German philosophy, he came under the influence of the later thought of Schelling. The German thinker saw philosophy of religion as arising within Christianity and as trying to understand Christian belief from within, and what Solovyev described as 'free theosophy' certainly bears some resemblance to Schelling's 'positive' philosophy, which he opposed to the allegedly 'negative' philosophy of Hegel. In any case when one reads Solovyev's speculative interpretation of the Trinity, it is

difficult to avoid the impression that what theologians have
been accustomed to describe as a mystery is being presented as
a conclusion in a metaphysics inspired by Neoplatonism and
German idealism.

The retort might be made that if, for a time at any rate,
Solovyev conceived 'true philosophy' as presupposing faith, it
was not so much a question of his transforming faith into
speculative metaphysics as of his pursuing theological thought
while labelling it 'philosophy'. This view of the matter,
however, seems to rest on the assumptions that Solovyev meant
by faith a set of propositions, of formulated Christian beliefs,
and that he regarded philosophy of religion at least as a sustained attempt to explore the implications of these beliefs. But
are the assumptions correct?

When, at an earlier date, Khomyakov asserted that faith
precedes the logical activity of reason, he meant by the word
'faith', as used in a general sense, immediate or intuitive apprehension of something as existing independently of the idea
of it in the human mind. As understood in this sense, faith is
common to all human beings. As for religious faith, understood
as intuitive apprehension of the existence of a supernatural
reality, this is shared, according to Khomyakov, by all genuine
members of a religiouis community. If philosophy is to provide
knowledge of a reality existing apart from our ideas, it must
presuppose faith in the first sense. If it is also to express what
Kireevsky called 'integral knowledge', it must presuppose faith
in the more specific sense of religious experience.

A substantially similar line of thought reappears in the
writings of Solovyev. If, he argues, experience is conceived as a
relation   between   an   epistemological   subject   and   a
phenomenon, it does not guarantee the extramental existence
of the phenomenal object. A mirage, experienced by a traveller
in the desert, is a phenomenal object, appearing to a subject,
but it is none the less a mirage. As for reasoning about concepts,
we are not entitled to assume without more ado that a given
concept is instantiated. For knowledge of existence a third
factor is required, which Solovyev describes sometimes as intellectual intuition and sometimes as faith. He also mentions
mystical knowledge as a necessary basis for an adequate philosophy, but the reference is to an immediate apprehension of the

reality of the Absolute, not to ecstasy or rapture or something of that kind.

Obviously, it is possible to call in question the claim that there is an intuitive grasp of extramental existence. To be sure, we all feel that there is a world existing independently of our conception of it; but some might wish to think in terms of Hume's theory of natural belief rather than to postulate an intellectual intuition, the possibility of which, as far as human beings are concerned, was denied by Kant, though reasserted by Schelling. For the matter of that, by the time that he came to write his last work, *Foundations of Theoretical Philosophy*, which he left unfinished at his death, Solovyev had come to think that an appeal to intuition was not sufficient, and that the claim to have experienced something as existing extramentally needed to be supported by reasoning.[2] But this does not affect the fact that if the word 'faith' is understood as referring to an alleged intellectual intuition of extramental existence, the idea of philosophy as presupposing faith does not warrant the conclusion that the philosophical thought in question should be described as pertaining to Christian theology.

Though, however, it is important to draw attention to Solovyev's use of the word 'faith' in the sense of intellectual intuition, it is clear that his thought as a whole presupposed and was inspired by a deep-seated Christian motivation. He did indeed insist that philosophy, considered as seeking objective truth, has no end beyond or outside itself,[3] and in his last work he remarked that as philosophical thought is an autonomous search for truth, an adherent of a positive religion can only hope that the philosopher will in fact arrive at conclusions which are in accord with the beliefs of the religion in question.[4] At the same time it would be unrealistic to represent Solovyev as prescinding altogether from his Christian beliefs when engaged in philosophical reflection. It is not as though he were concerned simply with problems in formal logic. If he insisted that philosophy is an autonomous search for truth, he also insisted that in relation to the human being's attainment of the goal of life (unity with God and others) philosophy is but one among a number of means. And there is certainly a sense in which Christian belief formed a framework for his thought.

It may seem that I have ascribed to Solovyev two incompatible lines of thought. But they can perhaps be united in more
or less the following way. The basic element in religion was, for
Solovyev, experience, or intuitive apprehension of the Absolute
as existing. Various religions have tried in their several ways to
express the content of religious experience. Christian thought
has endeavoured to give expression to basic Christian experience. This has resulted in the formulation of doctrinal
statements, which together form a framework for further reflection. But this framework should not be conceived as rigid,
unbending, fixed in immobility for all time. In Solovyev's
judgement, Russian Orthodox theology had become ossified,
excluding, as he put it, any free relationship between reason
and the content of religion.[5] In so far as he envisaged philosophy trying to penetrate religious beliefs with a view to understanding them better and expressing them in forms which
would have more meaning for people living in a cultural
context different from the one in which they were originally
formulated, the project would obviously be likely to evoke the
comment either that philosophy was taking the place of
theology or that the philosopher was practising theology under
the name of philosophy. However this may be, Solovyev had
another complaint against 'traditional theology', namely that it
failed to develop the content of religion in relation to empiric-
ally acquired knowlege, knowledge of nature for example.[6] He
was convinced that religion should cover the whole of life and
not withdraw or let itself be driven into a small hermetically
sealed compartment. We can say that he desired the development of an overall Christian *Weltanschauung* to the formation of
which philosophy, theology and other disciplines would contribute. Christian belief would form a framework for this process.
For example, belief in divine creation should stimulate study of
nature as intelligible. But the framework, as we have said,
should be conceived as something to be further and more
deeply understood. The process of understanding ought not to
be suspended at some given point, as Solovyev thought of the
Russian Church as trying to do.

Development of an overall interpretation of the world and
human life in the light of Christian faith would obviously
involve reflection on topics and problems lying beyond the field
of theology in the academic sense. For example, Solovyev's

epistemological theory was clearly a philosophical theory. Again, he was convinced that Christian faith should stimulate or evoke certain lines of social action. He deplored the fact that Christians in Russia had, for the most part, left the fight for social justice to a predominantly atheistic and materialist radical intelligentsia.

Mention was made above of the influence exercised on Solovyev's mind by the later philosophy of Schelling. We should remember, however, that after completing his studies in the University of Moscow, Solovyev had spent a year at the Zagorsk Theological Academy. When Kireevsky, then alienated from the Orthodox Church, was reading Schelling with the pious lady whom he had married in 1834, she remarked that the features of Schelling's thought which attracted her husband were all to be found in the writings of Greek Fathers of the Church, such as St Gregory of Nyssa. Kireevsky thereupon began to study patristic literature seriously. Solovyev too was well acquainted with the writings of the Fathers, and it is by no means fanciful to see in his thought a renewal of the efforts of the more speculatively inclined Fathers to interpret the world and human life and history in the light of Christian faith. The most eminent of the Latin Fathers, St Augustine, looked on Christianity as the true 'philosophy' or wisdom, which had succeeded the gropings and partial illumination of pre-Christian thought. True, the Fathers were quite capable of distinguishing between knowledge which could be gained without divine revelation and truths which, they believed, could be known only through revelation. At the same time they tended to think in terms of an overall Christian world-view rather than in terms of the sort of distinction between 'sacred doctrine' and philosophy, which was formulated later on, in the Middle Ages, notably by St Thomas Aquinas. The idea of seeing the world and all human life and history in the light of Christian belief is prominent in the thought of Solovyev.

The foregoing remarks were certainly not intended to suggest that Solovyev wished to blot out distinctions which had been made for good reasons. He was perfectly well aware, for example, not only that science had emerged from the complex area of inquiry once called 'philosophy' and that science itself had split into a plurality of disciplines, but also that this process had taken place for good reasons. He wanted to synthesize, to unite in one coherent world-view what had become divided, but not at the cost of confusing distinct disciplines. Solovyev called, for example, for a synthesis of science, philosophy and religion, but he obviously did not have in view obliteration of the distinction between empirical science and philosophy or between religion and science. What he aspired to do was to clarify the relations between science, philosophy and religion (which is not the same thing as theology, of course), so that the place of each in one coherent interpretation of types of human experience and activity might clearly appear. He believed that man's intellectual world had become fragmented, and he desired a restoration of unity. But if we choose to think of Solovyev as seeking to restore the intellectual unity exemplified in the writings of certain Fathers of the Church, we have to add that he wanted to restore this unity not as it once existed but as developed on a higher level, including in itself the complexity which had emerged in the course of intervening centuries.

Obviously, Solovyev used the word 'philosophy' in more than one sense. When he mentioned philosophy as something to be synthesized, he tended to mean the valuable elements in lines of thought which, taken simply by themselves, he regarded as one-sided, defective. In practice this meant that the basic truths in rationalism and empiricism needed to be subsumed and preserved in a more adequate philosophy. As for philosophy considered as a synthesizing activity, Solovyev referred to it sometimes as 'true philosophy' and sometimes as 'free theosophy'. It would combine the valuable elements in rationalism and empiricism with a third element, mentioned above, namely intellectual intuition or 'faith'.

Let us leave aside for the moment the idea of philosophizing in the light of faith and ask whether Solovyev's programme of synthesis, of developing a general interpretation of the world and human life, has any value or relevance today. It seems clear to me that it has. No sensible person would condemn synthesis as such. For it is an essential feature of understanding (not the only feature, of course) both in ordinary life and in science. It is doubtless true that large-scale synthesis is attended by a variety of risks, such as that of ignoring or slurring over differences in order to reach one's goal more speedily. Though, however, it would be absurd to demand that all philosophers should set about constructing world-views (the picture of them doing so is somewhat comical), the desire to achieve conceptual mastery over one's environment or over the world at large is natural enough. It has indeed to be recognized that anyone who attempts the construction of a general synthesis, of what would normally be considered a world-view, does so within a given historical situation, that the synthesis will be historically conditioned in a number of ways, and that no such world-view can be completely adequate, final and definite for all time. It may well be the case that the most valuable contributions to an ongoing process are made by philosophers who confine their attention to a limited area. For example, given the many possible ways of regarding the human being (from the angle of this or that science, as a moral agent, as enjoying aesthetic experience, and so on), a philosopher may focus his attention on outlining an overall view, one which would respect real distinction but would at the same time try to clarify the relations between, say, a scientific conception of the human being and the idea of the human being as a responsible moral agent. While, however, particular bits of synthesis, so to speak, are often engaged in by philosophers and may offer the best hope of valuable results, there does not seem to be any cogent reason for decreeing that synthesis must stop off at some particular point, proceeding no further.

It might, of course, be urged that though in past centuries, in the Middle Ages for example, large-scale synthesis may have seemed a perfectly reasonable goal at which to aim, this sort of enterprise is no longer practicable. Let us suppose, for example, that someone undertakes to show that the scientific and religious views of the human being are compatible and complimentary, each contributing to an overall, unified and coherent conception of the person. Is there such a thing as the scientific view of man, except perhaps as an ideal goal, the content of which we are not in a position to state? Before the philosopher could compare the scientific idea of the human being with the religious idea, he or she would have to develop a synthesizing scientific view derived from examination of the findings of a plurality of particular sciences. Further, scientific theories are subject to revision and change. Again, what is *the* religious view of the human being? It is possible to make the phrase more definite by substituting, for instance, 'Christian' for 'religious'. But even then it may not prove to be altogether easy to reach agreement about what constitutes the Christian view of the human being. In brief, while abstract talk about the desirability of synthesis may sound impressive, reflection on the complexity of the task should be sufficient to make clear its impracticable nature.

This line of objection doubtless helps to show the implausibility of any claim to have constructed or to be able to construct a comprehensive world-view or general interpretation of reality which is or would be final and complete. It does not follow, however, that serious attempts to exhibit, for instance, the interrelations between distinct types of human experience and forms of activity, with a view to developing a philosophical anthropology, are futile. If a synthesizing view of this kind is later found to need modification or even radical revision, this no more shows that its construction was futile or pointless than the fact that an astronomical theory is later shown to stand in need of revision proves that the initial formulation of the theory was simply wasted effort. The situation would obviously be different if it were assumed that the aim of philosophy is simply to formulate necessarily true propositions. But it should be clear that I am operating with a wider idea of the functions of philosophical thought.

It may be said that to try, for example, to exhibit the interrelations between distinguishable 'forms of life', to use a Wittgensteinian phrase, is not quite the same thing as to undertake construction of a world-view. But even if this is true, it might very well be a way of approaching development of a world-view. It would certainly be a way of attempting to restore that intellectual unity which, according to Solovyev, man was tending to lose or had already lost. In modern times philosophy has tended to take the form of philosophy of science, philosophy of history (meta-history), philosophy of religion, philosophy of mathematics, and so on. The present writer is sometimes strongly tempted to conclude that this state of affairs must simply be accepted, and that world-views and grandiose attempts at large-scale synthesis should be abandoned, relegated to past history. But the process of fragmentation can hardly fail to evoke a compensating call for correlation or synthesis in the interests of understanding, of obtaining conceptual mastery over the multiplicity of phenomena. It is not, for example, a question of trying to undo the emergence of newly recognized branches of empirical science. It is a question of trying to discern the relations between them, to form an overall view. Further, as was remarked above, it is hard to see any solid justification for demanding that the process of synthesis should be halted at a particular point, provided that going beyond this point does not mean going beyond the limits of intelligibility.

As for the idea of developing a world-view or synthesis in the light of Christian faith, when faith is understood as referring to basic Christian belief, it is difficult to see any cogent objection to this project, provided, of course, that there is no attempt to pass it off as an example of presuppositionless thought. To be sure, if someone is convinced that the Christian religion has had its day and should be left behind, he or she is unlikely to regard as worth while any expenditure of time and energy on contributing to the development of a general interpretation of the world and human life in the light of faith. If, however, one is prepared to give serious consideration to the possibility that Christian belief can contribute to understanding in a variety of areas, one can hardly condemn the endeavour to show that it does in fact possess this potentiality. It is true that the Christian religion came into the world as a gospel of salvation, not as a philosophical system or *Weltanschauung*. It is also true that a personal relationship to God and to other human beings lies at the heart of Christianity. But it by no means follows that any attempt to work out a synthesis in the light of Christian faith is to embark on a project contrary to the spirit of the Christian religion.

These remarks should not be understood as implying, for example, the claim that Christian faith can add to our scientific knowledge of the world. Given Christian belief in the creative activity of God, it can be inferred that creation is in principle intelligible. Christian belief is thus capable of stimulating the scientific study of nature and the human being; but scientific knowledge obviously has to be obtained by the use of scientific methods. If someone were inclined to maintain that the world is not in fact intelligible but that all alleged intelligibility is conferred by the human mind on what is in itself unintelligible, Christian faith would, I suppose, stimulate the person to question this theory and to persist in the quest for objective intelligibility; but it would not present him with any ready-made solution to his problem.

Consider for a moment construction of a philsophical anthropology. If a philosopher believes that religion is outmoded rubbish, he is unlikely to concern himself with synthesizing religious and scientific conceptions of the human being. He will doubtless think that in order to form a more adequate view of man any religious conception should be abandoned. If, however, a philosopher is a Christian believer, consistency demands that he should see more in man than, say, an object of scientific inquiry. But precisely how this 'more' should be conceived, and how the various aspects of the human being are related to one another are matters for his own reflection. To philosophize in the light of faith is not the same thing as to derive all the answers to questions from faith.

In the course of this essay reference has been made to the creation of a unified and coherent world-view. Honesty compels one to admit that we cannot form a completely adequate Christian world-view, inasmuch as Christian belief gives rise to problems to which it is unable to offer a theoretical solution which will put an end to all questioning. The problem of evil is an obvious example. The Christian religion, however, is not meant to solve all theoretical problems; it is turned towards life and conduct. It includes as an essential element certain basic and inbuilt judgements of value, acceptance of which is an integral feature of adherence to Christianity. To draw attention to the implications of these judgements in regard to human choice and action and to socio-political problems is an important part of thinking pursued in the light of faith. Solovyev was perfectly justified in emphasizing, if one may use a Marxian phrase, the relation between theory and practice. If some good Christians are apt to form hasty conclusions about what the Christian attitude or line of conduct in regard to some social or socio-political problem ought to be, this serves to draw attention to the need for serious and sustained thought, thought which can fairly be described as philosophizing in the light of Christian faith.

It may not be altogether irrelevant to remark that if a general interpretation of the world and human life in the light of religious faith were incapable of making any favourable impression on educated people today, it would hardly be considered necessary by the authorities in Solovyev's country to prevent, as far as they can, religiously inspired or orientated thought from exercising any influence in the cultural sphere. Any serious renewal of the movement started by Solovyev and carried on by his successors in the period preceding the First World War would clearly be regarded as posing a threat to the monopoly enjoyed by the officially sponsored ideology.

To conclude, Professor H.D. Lewis is both a Christian and a philosopher, and he has spent many years lecturing and writing in the field of philosophy of religion. If I have understood him correctly, he has maintained that there can be such a thing as an intellectual intuition not of God himself but of the necessity of God's existence. He has also proposed the view that the function of philosophy in the area of religion is to make more explicit for us the nature and status of the religious beliefs, if any, which we hold. Further, he has written extensively about the human person. Up to a point, therefore, he may feel some sympathy with some of the ideas mentioned in this essay. In any case it is both a privilege and a pleasure to have had the opportunity of contributing to a volume in honour of a distinguished philosopher and a former colleague in the University of London.

1 Sobranie Sochinenii, *Collected Works*, Brussels, 1966, IV, p.243. From the preface to *The History and Future of Theocracy*.
2 Ibid., IX, p.106, *Theoretical Philosophy*, 1.9.
3 Ibid., I, p.310, *Philosophical Principles*, 3.
4 Ibid., IX, p.95, *Theoretical Philosophy*, 1.4.
5 Ibid., II, p.349, *Critique of Abstract Principles*, 46.
6 Ibid.

Decision and Religious Belief

THOMAS McPHERSON

Does it make sense to talk of *deciding* to believe something? This question has been raised not infrequently by Hywel D. Lewis in his writings.[1]

The answer to the question, or so it seems to me, depends on the distance to which you are willing to throw your conceptual net. If you confine yourself to belief about matters of fact the answer may seem to be no. There are powerful arguments against the meaningfulness of the notion of deciding to believe factual propositions. Such arguments, however, make less deep an impression in the case of other — perhaps richer and more complex — areas, such as that of *religious* belief. If we take 'belief' as a general term covering a family whose members include commitment, assent, conviction, faith, etc., then there is no difficulty in finding cases where belief could be called a matter of the will; specifically, where we would be prepared to talk of someone deciding to believe something.

For reasons of literary style, if for no other reason, people move about between the term 'belief' and some of its near-synonyms. For a change from talking about someone's beliefs we may refer to his views, his opinions, his convictions, his suppositions, his principles, etc. Instead of using the expression 'believing *p*', we may say 'assenting to *p*', 'holding that *p*', 'having faith that *p*', 'assuming *p*', 'being of the opinion that *p*', 'deeming that *p*', 'judging that *p*', etc. A philosopher discussing belief may, of course, want to make a particular point of sticking to the terms 'belief', 'believe'. But some of those other expressions, just mentioned, certainly look as if they are located within the same general territory. And those expressions do not all seem to fit easily into a Humean picture of the necessary passivity of belief (e.g., 'assent to', 'deem that', 'judge that').

If then we take the term 'believe' in a sufficiently wide sense

I see no difficulty in holding that belief may sometimes be a matter of the will. But it is worth considering more closely what does seem to be the central kind of case; namely, where what we are concerned with is the term 'believe' itself rather than anything that might or might not be a near-synonym, and where what is believed is some more or less straightforward matter of fact. And I want to put the question: is it really true even of this central kind of case that belief is never an affair of the will? I think that even here there is room for the notion of *deciding* to believe.

Bernard Williams argues that I cannot 'bring it about' that I believe something (something, that is, in the area of straightforward matters of fact) because beliefs aim at truth, and 'if I could acquire a belief at will I could acquire it whether it was true or not', and, furthermore, 'I would know that I could acquire it whether it was true or not', so how could I really think of it as a belief, 'i.e., as something purporting to represent reality'?[2]

Now truth is indeed a constraint on belief. In particular, I am not free to decide to believe something that I know to be false.[3] But that would be an extreme case. Consider rather cases where the evidence (including testimony) that is available to us is limited or conflicting or confused, and we have to play our hunches, draw upon our experience, etc. Sometimes prompt action is needed and we cannot afford to wait for the evidence to become fuller, more consistent, clearer. We may have to decide to believe one thing rather than another because, although we are not certain that it is true, it seems the best bet, the most likely thing, quite probably true, etc., and because there is some good reason why we cannot leave the matter open. A jury may have to decide whose testimony to accept where witnesses conflict, and it seems natural to express this by saying that they decide to believe A rather than B or *p* rather than *q*. The young medical missionary in a remote area is far from indifferent to truth when he comes to the conclusion, somewhat desperately, that giving drug A rather than drug B will cure a seriously ill child. Flashbacks to teachers in conflict on the subject pass rapidly through his mind. He has never faced this disease before. There is no one to advise him now. What (and indeed whom) is he to believe? He decides to believe teacher X and drug A; or, we may say, he decides to believe that A is best.

It is often said that the notion that there is such a thing as deciding to believe must be a misunderstanding; that we deceive ourselves if we think that we literally decide to believe something: for what happens is rather that we come to the conclusion that something is probably the case, and we are simply misdescribing such a situation if we say that we have decided to believe that thing. On this reading, supposing we take the medical missionary case, the correct thing to say would not be, as I have just said, that the young man decides to believe that drug A will succeed, but rather that he decides that drug A will succeed. But surely he is in no position to decide any such thing. What he can decide is to put his faith in one thing rather than another. He decides to *believe* that drug A will cure the child. If he did not he would have difficulty in justifying giving it to the child. I do not find that this suggestion about misunderstanding offers a satisfactory way of disposing of the notion of deciding to believe. Cases like those that I have mentioned are cases where the expression 'decide to believe' would, I think, be a proper one to use, and in such cases one is certainly saying more than that something is probably the case.

A reductionist attitude (if we may call it that) to the notion of deciding to believe is no doubt encouraged if a person sees that notion as belonging in the same box as certain other, probably objectionable, notions. Bernard Williams, at the end of his paper, makes some remarks about the notion of wanting to believe something, and gives the example of someone whose son has very probably been drowned and who 'very much wants to believe that his son is alive'.[4] It is in cases where we might be inclined to use phrases like 'wanting to believe', 'making himself believe', 'persuading himself to believe', 'bringing it about that he believes' (which last phrase is in fact the phrase used by Williams in the passage which I referred to earlier) that we may well feel that the constraint of truth on belief is in danger of being lost. But there is, alongside these, a perfectly innocent kind of deciding to believe, the kind that you have in the sort of situation that I have tried to describe — where we think something is probably true and where we see the circumstances as requiring us (or at any rate leading us) to adopt it in advance of certainty. 'I have decided to believe your story', says the headmaster to the plausible pupil who, unlikely as his story is, quite possibly is telling the truth — and, anyway, there are more important things for headmasters to do than inquire into the truth of a pupil's story beyond a certain point. Of course, there are other reasons why people decide to believe things. For example, it may strike us that a life lived without believing a particular thing would be so very unpleasant that we had better believe it. The consequences of defeat in a war may be, as people say, 'unthinkable', so people decide to believe that defeat is impossible. Again, there are people who have a frame of mind such that they are disposed to put a bad interpretation on what other people do: we may say that they have decided to believe the worst of others. People may decide to *subscribe to* a particular set of beliefs which could include factual beliefs (e.g., 'suffered under Pontius Pilate').[5]

What are the likely effects on a person's appreciation of religious belief of his holding assumptions like the following: (a) belief in matters of fact is the standard or central kind of belief and it is necessarily passive; (b) if belief ever is an affair of the will that probably means that it is a matter of trying to make yourself believe something that you suspect is not true? Religious belief sometimes involves decision. On such assumptions as those just mentioned, religious belief may quite possibly appear at best an odd, off-beat kind of belief, and at worst arbitrary and irrational in a particularly unattractive way. Some people (who are perhaps not much attracted to religion anyway) might be led to see religious belief as probably not worth a rational person's serious attention, or, it may be, confirmed in that view. Other people (religiously-minded people, this time, and people who happen also to want to preserve a link between religious belief and truth) may be led to play down the element of decision in religious belief, which element they may see as weakening religious belief, and disposed perhaps towards making religious belief conform as much as possible to factual belief.

But if deciding to believe is kept separate from notions of making oneself believe something one knows or thinks to be not true, and if, furthermore, even the standard or central case of belief (factual belief) can, despite well-known arguments to the contrary, itself be seen as sometimes allowing for an element of deciding to believe, then one kind of motive for rejecting religious belief and one kind of motive for seeing religious belief in an incomplete way are both removed.

It is perhaps worth reminding ourselves that the connection between belief and truth has to include a place for self-verifying beliefs, like the case of the athlete whose strong belief that he can win is an important cause of his winning. It is obviously useful in many walks of life, supposing you want something to happen, to be able to put yourself into the frame of mind of believing that it will happen (e.g., 'I believe in order to understand. For this also I believe, — that unless I believed, I should not understand' — Anselm, *Proslogion*, chapter I.)

One important reason for resisting attempts to rule out the possibility of deciding to believe is the following. If we deny this possibility then it will become more difficult to maintain the proposition that people are sometimes properly to be held responsible for their beliefs (including factual beliefs), that people are properly to be praised or blamed for believing or not believing certain things. The religious application of this needs no explicit pointing out; again, let us rather consider the (presumably more controversial) case of factual belief, discussing this now together with two other kinds of belief.

People believe many things that they ought not to believe. A person may believe something that is at variance with facts about society or the world that anybody in his position should be expected to know. Or he may believe something that he ought not to believe because it is inconsistent with a fundamental set of things that he also believes. Or he may believe, for example, that Hitler was right to try to exterminate the Jews, and he ought not to believe that. So, for commonsensical (factual), logical or moral reasons we may want to say that someone ought not to believe something that he believes.

In saying this we are, no doubt, partly intending to condemn people's failure to make an appropriate degree or kind of effort. That is, we are, in part, blaming them for not trying hard enough — not trying hard enough to find out the sort of thing that people in their position can be expected to know, not trying hard enough to be consistent, not trying hard enough to face up to the demands of morality. But I think it would be a mistake to say that all that is involved is failure of effort of this kind. Of course, if belief can never be an affair of the will then what we would be condemning in such cases would, indeed, have to be something other than the person's believing something, and the obvious candidate is failure of effort on his part of the kinds mentioned. But there is more to it than such failure of effort.

When we rebuke someone for bad logic, part of what we are rebuking him for will often, no doubt, be failure of effort. But 'You ought not to believe *p*' is not saying (in the appropriate case) 'You ought to try harder to avoid inconsistency'. Failure to try hard enough to avoid inconsistency has no doubt contributed importantly to his believing *p*, but what we are rebuking him for is believing *p*. That is what we have said. A man may feel remorse for having believed something; another may regret that so much of his life was spent in the darkness of ignorance or unbelief (this does not have to be religious unbelief; it could be factual ignorance: people regret having missed a Classical or a musical education). Such feelings are not fully to be accounted for by saying that these people are condemning themselves for not having tried hard enough to get the facts right or to learn more: they may not even have been in a position to try at all. Resisting belief, rejecting beliefs, committing oneself to something, etc., involve the will; but in a more complex way than is exhausted in notions like trying to be consistent, trying to find things out.

Take the story (which would come under the heading of cases of failure in commonsense) of the gentleman who approached the Duke of Wellington and, presumably having mistaken him for George Jones RA, said 'Mr Jones, I believe', to which the Duke replied, 'Sir, if you believe that you will believe anything.' In what way was the gentleman at fault? No doubt there was an element of not trying hard enough. Any gentleman, one might say, could be expected to have made himself more familiar with those distinctive features, that distinguished bearing. There was an inappropriateness in thinking that the name 'Mr Jones' could be applied to, of all people, the great Arthur Wellesley, Duke of Wellington. But what the Duke was objecting to was the gentleman's own phrase.[6] The gentleman ought not to have believed that he was addressing Mr Jones; and that is not merely a matter of whether he had in the past tried hard enough to learn various facts. He is being rebuked, it seems, for having a certain belief, not for the way in which he may have come to hold it or to fail to reject it.

The moral case is particularly important. 'You ought not to believe that Hitler was right.' Does this mean only that you ought to have tried harder to learn your moral lessons? Does it even mean this at all?

The effect of holding that belief can never be an affair of the will is to make it more difficult for us to praise and blame people for what they believe, or to say that people ought or ought not to believe certain things. But it is a matter of some importance to be able to do this. It is a matter bound up with respect for human beings, and with self-respect. We should feel uneasy if someone were to say: 'My beliefs are, of course, not under my control; I cannot help it if I believe that Hitler was right, that you are Mr Jones, that cruelty to animals is always wrong but that fox-hunting is an admirable pursuit: you are never entitled to condemn me for believing what I believe' (or praise me either, he would no doubt have to add).

The responsibility of people for some at least of their beliefs seems to me a matter of fundamental importance in our judgements about human beings. To the extent that the notion of deciding to believe is clearly sympathetic to (to put it no higher) the view that people can appropriately be held responsible for some of their beliefs then the notion of deciding to believe is worth defending. Not all our beliefs are things over which we have no control. Our beliefs (at any rate the most interesting among them) do not just happen to us. The tendency is to think of beliefs as passive furniture of the mind to be discussed in terms of their truth and falsehood, their compatibility with one another, etc. But beliefs are held by people; and how did they get into people's minds in the first place? Effort will sometimes (not always) have been involved: people work away in laboratories, they slave over books in libraries, they memorize lists of words or dates. We could think in terms of a single package consisting of a belief in a person's mind together with the work that may have been put in towards his arriving at it, or indeed that may be involved now in his retaining it against the distractions of other interests, the actions of brainwashers, or (more prosaically) failing memory. And as well as a past and a present, a person's beliefs have consequences. These consequences, too, can be looked at as part of the single package. When a professional man's judge-

ment turns out to have been at fault what are we blaming him
for? The patient's death, the rampant woodworm, the bill
from the Inland Revenue? Yes; but not separately from either
his negligence (or whatever it should be called) or his believing certain things he ought not to have believed. If the
negligence was avoidable by him, and if he is properly to be
blamed for the consequence, we might as well make him
responsible for the middle stage of believing *p* as well. I express
this perhaps rather flippantly, but the important point is that
we take our fellow human beings more seriously if we are
prepared to hold them responsible for some of their beliefs
(even their factual beliefs) than if we hold them responsible
for none, and then it becomes a matter of where the line of
responsibility is to be drawn.

I began by mentioning the contrast between a wider and a
narrower way of looking at the notion of belief, a contrast in
terms of which such things as religious belief are located some
way out from the conceptual middle ground occupied by the
standard or central kind of belief, namely, factual belief. But
there is, of course, no reason why the notion of factual belief
itself should not be looked at in a wider or in a narrower
perspective: matters of fact are of varied kinds. Just as the
standard or central case of belief seems to be factual belief so
the standard or central case of factual belief seems to be belief
in the most simple kind of positive empirical fact (of the cat-
sitting-on-the-mat variety). But in works of imagination something that is physically or even logically impossible can be
presented as fact. Matters of fact include negative facts and
hypothetical facts; predictions can be announced as facts; well-
supported theories are often called facts. We distinguish historical facts from linguistic facts or botanical facts. We talk of
'brute' facts, presumably intending a contrast with gentler,
more elusive facts. There are firm facts and evanescent facts;
persistent facts, recurring facts, unique facts.

We may note in particular that calling a belief 'factual' is
sometimes a way of saying that it is to be taken literally;
and sometimes a way of saying that it is true. Are the beliefs that
Jesus is Son of God, or that God loves us, *factual* beliefs? I think
that some would assert that they are with as much force as
others would use in denying that they could possibly be. It is

safe to say, though, that on an interpretation of 'factual belief' wide enough for religious beliefs to be included among factual beliefs we should be in danger of losing the point of the *contrast* between factual belief and the 'richer and more complex areas' of belief within which, as I claimed at the beginning, religious belief is to be found: some of the contents of these richer and more complex areas would turn out to be just yet more factual beliefs — only, no doubt, in a 'richer and more complex' sense of 'factual'.

To describe religious belief as not factual sometimes seems to be intended to point a kind of fault or shortcoming in it. Alasdair MacIntyre has argued that since (as he holds) if a belief is chosen it cannot be a factual belief, a view of Christian belief that sees it as capable of being chosen would entail that 'the truths of Christian orthodoxy must be regarded as something other than factual in kind'.[7] In its context the suggestion seems to be that this conclusion ought to be unwelcome to a Christian believer. Presumably it would indeed be unwelcome to any believer for whom 'other than factual' carried the meaning 'not true'; and it would also be unwelcome to at least some of those for whom 'other than factual' meant 'not to be taken literally'. On the other hand, if a belief's being non-factual meant merely that it is not an empirical belief, no serious and intelligent Christian believer would be disturbed by being told that Christian beliefs are not factual; such a believer never thought that they were factual, in that sense (or, at any rate, not the most important among them). It is far from obvious that it constitutes an objection to a view of Christian beliefs to say that that view holds or implies that Christian beliefs are not 'factual'. In any case, that it is chosen does not entail either that a belief is untrue or that it is not to be taken literally. So MacIntyre's argument, if it is indeed intended as a criticism of what he calls 'modern Christian theology', does not make its point as far as any of the three senses of 'factual' that I have just referred to is concerned — and they seem the natural ones to take into account here.[8] What I am saying is entirely obvious; namely, that what we mean by 'factual' is an important part of this whole matter.

I have remarked that whatever may be the case with factual belief it is uncontroversial that as far as religious belief is concerned it is possible to *decide* to believe. But although I believe it uncontroversial, some of my readers may, of course, disagree. At any rate, something more should be said about how exactly decision enters into religious belief. It has been suggested to me that at the heart of all religions there is a decision; and no doubt a religion could be seen as something which, whatever else it is, has as its foundation a single decision — a decision to leave home, to adopt a new style of life, to follow or 'accept' Jesus, etc. I do not know whether this account of the religions of the world can be sustained. If it should turn out that in the case of some religions the alleged foundational decision is too metaphorical in character then, of course, the account would cease to be very illuminating. But it seems to apply to Christianity on a certain kind of understanding of it ('Make your decision for Christ this very day', the evangelical preacher says) which would make the claim to be going back to the most basic sort of Christianity.

I suspect, however, that many Christian believers may be unhappy with the terms 'decision' and 'decide' precisely because they seem to suggest some kind of instantaneous event. 'Christianity', such believers might say, 'whether we like it or not, is not an undeveloped religion; attempts to go back to its alleged primitive heart only distort it. What we may sometimes think of disparagingly as unwanted accretions of doctrine and the like are in fact, if we are sensible about it, clearly part of what Christianity by now is. It makes no sense to think of someone *deciding* to be a Christian if that means making a single decision on some particular occasion: such a decision could never take in all that it would need to.'

The notion of 'deciding' to believe does, indeed, seem to suggest a picture of someone adopting a belief on some datable occasion. And this will strike some people who think of themselves as religious believers as simply not true to their own experience. A believer who is not aware of any particular turning point in his own religious life, and who is all too aware of the detail and difficulty of much Christian belief, may well consider that the notion of deciding to believe has little to do with his own religion. He might prefer to say that religious belief is something that a person needs to grow into, perhaps after setting himself to develop in a certain direction. The decision 'to believe' might be looked on as a decision not to resist any longer certain influences, or a decision to devote time to reflection on certain writings, or to try to enter more whole-heartedly into certain ritual practices, etc.; belief may be thus induced, or may thus grow to seem more surely founded.

I do not question that this account would fit the situation of some religious believers. My objection to it will, however, be obvious in the light of the earlier part of this paper. What we have here is, once again, the sort of account, already discussed, where the exercise of will in connection with belief is located in the process of effort that may lead up to belief. But my theme is 'deciding to believe', not 'deciding to set oneself to believe', or 'deciding to try to believe', let alone 'deciding to read the Bible', or 'deciding to go to church more often' or 'deciding to avoid my jeering atheist acquaintances'.

It is, of course, perfectly true that religious belief may be something a person grows up with, and grows into, and in the case of some believers there may not be any event that a believer wants to point to as the very moment when he became a religious believer. It is understandable that someone who might be perfectly prepared to see religious belief as a matter of the will — prepared, for example, to use terms like 'commit-ment' in giving an account of it — should still want to resist the terms 'decide' or 'decision'; it is the suggestion of something happening in an instant that makes these latter words seem not to fit the case. If the believer happens also to be a philosopher he may have an added reason for resisting these terms; they may seem to imply an exploded theory of belief — an occur-rence theory — rather than a more fashionable disposition theory.

But although this resistance is understandable, it is not jus-tified. Beliefs may have a beginning and an end, and there are cases where there is not the slightest difficulty in dating the beginning of someone's conversion to something quite complex, like socialism or monetarism, or in dating his abandoning of it. That there are also cases where such dating is difficult or impossible should not lead us to ignore the cases where dating is possible and proper. And as for theories of belief, a dis-positional account of belief does not rule out beliefs having beginnings: there might be a sort of occurrence, a decision

marking the beginning of belief in something, and thereafter
the believing could be explained in dispositional terms.
However, it is no part of my present purpose to discuss general
theories of belief.

Decision enters into religious belief in various ways. Certainly it is possible for someone to decide to set himself to acquire
belief; and it is possible for him later, having become a believer,
to recall himself to his belief from time to time by acts of
decision when that belief seems to be weakening. Decisions of
these kinds, as we have noted already, are, of course, improper-
ly called decisions *to believe*; but they do not exhaust the ways
in which decision may enter into religious belief. My concern
has been with what it is proper to call decision *to believe*. There
are certainly instances of this in religion. An insistence upon the
reality of deciding to believe does not have to go along with a
denial of the other dimensions of decision in relation to belief
that have just been mentioned: indeed, it would be absurd to
deny them. But equally there is no need to suppose that
deciding to believe must always be explicable in terms of these
other dimensions. All may find a place in the account of religious belief. The noting of these various dimensions of decision
(within which, furthermore, there can be a multiplicity of
particular decisions) may go some way to meet the objection
that 'decision' carries too much the suggestion of an instantaneous event. A person's religious belief may be built up on
many decisions, of different kinds, and perhaps often repeated.
But among them it is proper to allow a place for decisions *to
believe*.

1 A recent instance is H.D. Lewis, *Freedom and Alienation*, Scottish Academic
  Press, Edinburgh, 1985, pp.46–7.
2 Bernard Williams, 'Deciding to Believe', in *Problems of the Self*, Cambridge
  University Press, 1973, p.148.
3 Or am I?

    He smiled at her so enchantingly that Susan had to capitulate.
    "All right," she grumbled, "I'll believe you even when I know it's a
    lie"

  — Aldous Huxley, *Time Must Have a Stop*, Chatto and Windus, London,
  1945, p.18.

4 Williams, op cit., pp.149–50.
5 Something of an odd man out among the largely 'metaphysical' phrases of the Apostles' Creed.
6 Of course, 'I believe', in sentences like 'Mr Jones, I believe' is often just a conventional noise (like the rather foolish 'I presume' in 'Dr Livingstone, I presume') made to soften what would otherwise be a blunt barking out of a proper name. But the Duke, in the present case, is clearly taking it seriously.
7 Alasdair MacIntyre and Paul Ricoeur, *The Religious Significance of Atheism*, Columbia University Press, New York, 1969, p.23.
8 What MacIntyre says of 'the dogmas of Christian orthodoxy' is: 'For these dogmas are, or at least were, intended to be taken as factual truths in the same sense that it is a matter of fact whether or not tomorrow will bring rain' — op. cit., p.23. This — with its reference to the future — seems an odd sense of 'factual' to cite in connection with traditional Christian dogmas.

Religious Experience

T.A. ROBERTS

I

A great deal has been written by philosophers of religion, including H.D. Lewis most notably in his *Our Experience of God*,[1] on the topic of religious experience, but some questions still remain to puzzle and bewitch us.

Discussion of religious experience can profitably focus on two main aspects, that associated with public events and that associated with an individual's solitary experience. I shall refer to the former as religious experience (A) and the latter as religious experience (B).

To say that religious experience (A) can be manifested in and through public events is, on the surface, a valid and a straightforward claim. Religious experience can then be defined as 'experiencing public events "religiously" by sharing a community life with the appropriate emotions'.[2] Unless the definition is to be taken in too broad a sense, 'public events' needs some restriction or qualification. A person attending an international rugby match at Cardiff Arms Park and hearing the crowd sing Cwm Rhondda with *hwyl* and fervour is moved with emotion, almost to tears. Does this count as a religious experience? In the context of his discussion Clark implicitly restricts the notion of 'experiencing public events religiously' to the context of worship, that is public events which constitute the 'rituals' of religion, the services of worship as commonly experienced in branches of the Christian Church in the West. For the Anglican Church in England and the Church of Scotland, such religious services constitute the 'national religion'. As a member of the community, a person is intimately related to this national religion by having the great turning points in his or her life — marriage, baptism of a child, burial of a relative — sanctified by the services of the Church. The community at large finds its unity and identity strengthened by having crucial events in the life of the community hallowed by the Church — a coronation of a monarch, the wedding of a royal personage and the national services of commemoration for those who died in two world wars.

Allowing, as Clark righly maintains, that such 'public events' which provide the context for religious experience, are set within a particular and identifiable religious tradition, Clark holds that the important question to ask is not 'do you think it is true?' but 'do you find it touches on your life?' The criteria which Clark lays down for answering the question of whether it touches on your life are: does the religious ritual arouse the appropriate emotions, and are these emotions carried over into one's ordinary life? Clark's examples of emotions which are aroused by religious experience are 'confident expectation', 'communal reassertion of high courage against adversity', 'grief', 'heroic joy' and 'immortal love'. Religious experience is defective if these emotions do not influence the worshipper's ordinary life. Indeed on Clark's analysis there seem to be two possible defects: the worshipper feels too little of the appropriate emotions, and so the emotions fail to affect his everyday life; or the worshipper feels these emotions too much so that 'he will earn the vague dislike of his compatriots if he is too obviously happy, too much inclined to uncomplaining courage and affectionate joy'.[3]

Reflection on this aspect of Clark's analysis of religious experience[4] raises two comments. For him, the focus of public religious experience seems to be those religious events which constitute the great occasions, when the national religion is the instrument for focussing the attention and mood of the community on some national event of great moment, for example, religious services of thanksgiving to God for the victory of British arms in the Falklands. Those 'public events', the ordinary church services to which the worshipper has constant access and which are not identified, except perhaps through prayers for Queen and Parliament, with high events of state, seem to be left out of the account. Yet these are the 'staple diet', that which nourishes and sustains the spiritual life of the worshipper. Moreover, to define religious experience, in terms of those 'public events which arouse the appropriate emotions' lands Clark in difficulties. There is first a possible inconsistency in his account. 'True piety' he writes 'is to honour our obligations and keep on till the end, without misleading assistance from the sort of spurious affection, drunken excitement and ignorant pride that is evoked, in some, by ritual'.[5] This raises the question of whether 'honouring our obligations' which constitutes, for Clark, true piety, can be achieved without experiencing the 'appropriate emotions' constitutive of religious experience, as defined by Clark. Does Clark wish to maintain that 'experiencing the appropriate emotions' of religious experience (A) is a necessary or sufficient condition of true piety or can true piety be achieved without experiencing sudden emotions? Another obvious difficulty in Clark's analysis is the danger of slipping into the claim that since religious experience (A) essentially involves 'the appropriate emotions' the aim and object of the public events which are the ground of this religious experience is precisely to arouse these emotions. Two things are in danger of following from this. A worshipper attends a religious service in the hope of experiencing certain emotions and is then naturally disappointed if no such emotions are experienced. If causally arousing certain emotions in the individual is the main aim of ritual, then in many instances, at least in the West, religious ritual conspicuously fails to achieve its intended effect. It leaves the worshipper stone cold. Alternatively the religious ritual may fail to arouse the 'appropriate emotions' but may succeed all too well in arousing 'spurious' emotions. Clark is well aware of this difficulty for all too often, he writes, our rituals arouse

> the sort of jolly, uncomprehending, transient romanticism that is to be found in nurse-meets-doctor fictions, soft-core pornography or military songs. A religious experience is one that brings easy tears to the eyes, makes the victim hot and cold, provides an orgasm without need to fear the consequences. Religious experience, in short, is often something that genuinely pious, God-fearing persons should beware . . . Charismatic revivalism is often as distrusted by ecclesiastics as by atheists, and much of the church's organization is directed towards controlling, not evoking, 'transports of delight'.[6]

A further possible weakness in Clark's account is that by associating religious experience (A) both with expressions of community solidarity and also the arousing and experiencing of the appropriate emotions, it denies religious experience to a person who fulfills the first requirement but not the second. A prominent public figure dies. Jones attends his funeral; in this he expresses his solidarity with his community by participating in the ritual of the church service. But he feels no particular emotions. The public figure was no close or personal friend and so he feels no grief. He has a vague awareness or sense of loss to the community of one who had served it well. He leaves the church in the conviction — not the feeling — that he has done the right thing by the community in attending the burial service as a mark of respect. On Clark's analysis, Jones's attendance at the burial service was not the occasion for religious experience, for he failed to feel the 'appropriate emotions'. This is certainly a consequence of Clark's definition of religious experience, which may suggest his definition is too restrictive.

A final brief observation. Whereas Clark stresses that aspect of religious experience (A) which is an expression of the unity, co-operation and integrity of the community, his discussion of religious experience (A) is individualistic; it is how (with appropriate emotions) the individual responds to certain public events, i.e. the ritual. One can envisage communities in which the ritual is enacted in order to secure the preservation and continuation of the community, with no emphasis being placed on how the participating individuals respond (emotionally or otherwise) to the public events. This implies that Clark's individualist approach to religious experience (A) is only one possible approach.

II

I wish to turn now to an examination of religious experience (B), the solitary experience of the individual on which is based a claim to have evidence for the existence of God.

Consider the following thesis, taken from H.H. Price's discussion of John Hick's 'eschatological verification thesis'.[7]

A spiritual person (in heaven) is able to discern facts which the non-spiritual person is unable to be aware of: these facts are empirical facts constituting evidence of the existence of God. As Price correctly observes, this thesis assumes that 'a person who has acquired certain conative and emotional dispositions is able to have experiences disclosing facts to him which others are unable to discern'.[8] These conative and emotive dispositions are in part moral, that is, the spiritual person is at the least a very good person. Moral goodness then is a necessary condition of being a spiritual person able to discern facts constituting evidence for God's existence. Price suggests that moral goodness is not a necessary and sufficient condition of spirituality. The sufficient condition being 'devotional practices', either public and outward, or private and inward. Price stresses the 'private and inward' devotional practices within a religious tradition, for these presuppose the validity of the claim that 'what a person is capable of being aware of depends in some degree upon the kind of person he is'.[9] The underlying assumption here is that every human being has certain capacities — let us call them spiritual capacities for lack of a better term — which remain latent and unactualized in most of us unless steps are taken to develop them. It could be argued that in modern Western technological society the average man's spiritual capacities, despite his maturity in other respects, are far less developed spiritually than for men in the Middle Ages.

Locating the 'spiritual' man in the world and not in heaven as with Hick, the thesis then runs as follows. A spiritual man is one who has experiences which unspiritual men do not have, and cannot have until their latent spiritual capacities are developed. The spiritual man's experiences are mainly, though not entirely, cognitive. They provide evidence for certain important propositions, evidence unspiritual persons are unable to have.[10] This evidence concerns the existence of God and his attitudes, and support for the proposition that God loves us.

Let us call the two versions of the thesis 'the Hick version' and 'the Price version'. The Hick version, in postulating the existence of heaven, makes a further claim about the existence of heaven which needs independent corroboration if the thesis is to be accepted.

The Price version is unencumbered by claims postulating the existence of heaven. This version posits the existence, in some

spheres, (not in the sphere for example of ordinary sense perception) of a relation between a man's cognitive powers and his
conative and emotional dispositions. One implication of this
view, as Price points out, is that 'the postulate of unrestricted
public verifiability' might be false. In the sphere of religion,
unless we are as charitable as the Good Samaritan, we are
unable to discern those empirical facts which are evidence for
God's existence. The claim that our cognitive powers depend
on the kind of person we are — straightforwardly false in the
case of ordinary perception — receives support from one sphere
very closely related to the religious, but to be distinguished from
it, namely the moral. Price's example is:

> if we are ourselves very selfish or unkind, there will be facts we
> shall not be able to notice . . . And so we move in the world of
> personal relations like blind men, unable to grasp what is going
> on around us. Here our moral defects do restrict our cognitive
> powers.[11]

The Price thesis can thus be summed up: unless we acquire
certain moral virtues, especially charity, cultivated by devotional practices, we shall not be capable of having certain sorts
of *cognitive* experiences, experiences essential for the verification
of religious claims.

There seems to be a further thesis lurking within the Price
thesis. This is the subsidiary thesis that unless one becomes as
charitable as the Good Samaritan, one does not fully understand what charity is, but having acquired the virtue, one
understands what the proposition 'God loves us' really means,
and in understanding it one sees that God exists. This subsidiary thesis makes the acquisition of the moral virtue of charity
a necessary condition of possessing these cognitive powers
which enable one to perceive the fact of God's existence.

With regard to Price's main thesis, which is an epistemological thesis, it is clearly suggested that evidence of God's existence
can only be discerned by those possessing certain cognitive
powers, and that these in turn are the consequence of acquiring
or developing certain conative and emotive dispositions. But
granting that it is true that there exists this relationship
between certain conative and emotional dispositions and those

cognitive powers which enable one to discern evidence of God's existence, one still requires from the 'spiritual person' a description of the evidence his special cognitive powers have acquired so that 'unspiritual' persons can examine and evaluate it. Price does not attempt to provide such evidence, so that his main thesis falls into the category of one that may possibly be true, and not one which has been established to be true.

Of Price's subsidiary thesis, clearly a full understanding of charity or agape will enable one to understand to some extent the nature of God's love. But this does not establish God's existence: it merely establishes the hypothetical proposition, if there is a God who loves us, his love is of this nature (agapeistic).

III

An attempt to explicate religious experience (B) without recourse to Price's appeal to the special cognitive powers which supervene upon certain acquired conative and emotional dispositions has been made by Richard Swinburne, but as I hope to show, his analysis, although not vulnerable to the criticism one can level at the Price thesis, is not entirely convincing.

Swinburne describes an experience as 'a conscious mental going-on', which may be described in such a way as to entail the existence of some particular thing or entity, external to and independent of the subject, beyond his stream of consciousness, a thing or entity it is an experience of; or it may be described in such a way as to carry no such entailment.[12] Thus if I have a mental (perceptual) experience which I describe as 'hearing a coach outside the window' I give, according to Swinburne, an external description. But if I describe my experience as having an auditory sensation which seemed to come from a coach outside the window, I give an internal description, for the description does not entail the existence of anything external of which the experience was purportedly an experience.

Swinburne points out that persons reporting their religious experiences 'often give external descriptions of them', for example 'I talked to God last night'. On this Swinburne comments:

> the trouble with taking any external description as the premiss of an argument from religious experience (to the existence of God) is that there is going to be considerable doubt about the truth of the premiss . . . So it seems natural to say, all arguments from religious experience must be phrased as arguments from experiences given internal descriptions.[13]

Normally an internal description is couched in the form 'the room seemed to be going round and round' or 'the carpet appeared to be blue' (Swinburne's examples).

Swinburne then invokes the distinction between the epistemic and comparative uses of verbs such as 'seems', 'appears', 'looks'. Here Swinburne is indebted to R. Chisholm's *Perception* (1957). If one says, 'the stick looks crooked in the water' this is the comparative or non-epistemic sense; if one says 'the carpet looks red' this is the epistemic use. Appealing to this distinction, Swinburne writes that the concept of 'religious experience' in its ordinary use can be usefully defined as an 'experience which seems (epistemically) to the subject to be an experience of God (either of his just being there, or doing, or bringing about something) or of some other supernatural thing'.[14]

The crucial feature of this definition is that what makes an experience religious is the way it seems to the subject.[15] Thus the agent seems to have an awareness of God even if the awareness is not necessarily mediated via the normal senses. Swinburne's next move is to invoke the causal theory of perception. Thus,

> S perceives X (believing that he is so doing) if and only if an experience of it seeming (epistemically) to S that X was present was caused by X's being present. So S has an experience of God if and only if its seeming to him that God is present is in fact caused by God being present.[16]

Another distinction made by Swinburne is that between public and private perceptions. A public perception is one when

> an object X may be such as to cause all persons rightly positioned who with certain sense-organs and certain concepts pay a certain degree of attention to have the experience of it seeming to them

that X is present . . . . But there may be objects O which cause
certain persons to have the experience of its seeming to them that
O is there without their having that affect on all other attentive
persons who occupy similar positions and have similar sense-
organs and concepts.[17]

In the latter case the perception of O is a private perception.
Religious experiences are normally private perceptions. Thus
one person can have a religious experience in circumstances
and in conditions in which his neighbour, equally attentive and
equally well equipped with sense-organs, does not have the
experience.

Having outlined his typical classes of religious experiences,
Swinburne then raises the crucial question, what is the eviden-
tial value of these religious experiences? Here he appeals to the
principle of credulity.

> It is a principle of rationality that (in the absence of special
> considerations) if it seems (epistemically) to a subject that X is
> present, then probably X is present: what one seems to perceive
> is probably so. How things seem to be is good grounds for a belief
> about how things are. From this it would follow that, in the
> absence of special considerations, all religious experiences ought
> to be taken by their subjects as genuine, and hence as substantial
> grounds for belief in the existence of their apparent object —
> God, or Mary, or Ultimate Reality of Poseidon.[18]

Swinburne notes that the principle is so phrased that how
things seem positively to be is evidence of how they are, whereas
how things seem not to be is not such evidence. If it seems to me
that there is no table in the room (Swinburne's examples
p. 255) this is not evidence for there being no table unless I have
taken steps to examine the room thoroughly. Similarly an
atheist who claims to have had an experience of there being no
God cannot claim this as evidence unless he has been able to
dispute successfully the claims to the existence of God.

Swinburne discusses attempts to so restrict the principle of
credulity so as to exclude its application to claims of religious
experience. He aims to show that such attempts are unjustified
and unsuccessful. I do not propose here to examine critically
Swinburne's attempt to refute those who hold that the principle
of credulity does not apply to religious experiences.

In introducing Swinburne's discussion of religious experience it was claimed that his analysis is unsatisfactory. This claim must now be substantiated. Let us accept Swinburne's initial premiss that all experience is ultimately based on mental goings-on. A sub-class of these mental goings-on are perceptions. Perceptions can be given, according to Swinburne, either an external or internal description. Consider the external description of a particular perception which is:

(1) 'I see a table'

This particular perception, an item in a particular agent's stream of consciousness, is a 'public perception', since, on another of Swinburne's distinctions, it is a perception of an object (the table) of which others can have perceptions (mental goings-on). The causal theory of perception links up here, for there exists the external object, the table, which causes the perception described by (1).

Consider now the following:

(2) 'I saw God'

Swinburne rules out this external description because it is not acceptable as a premiss of an argument from a religious experience to the existence of God, for if one sees God, then clearly God exists, and no argument is needed. Moreover there is considerable doubt, according to Swinburne, as to the truth of this premiss. Disallowing external descriptions of religious experiences, Swinburne then concentrates his analysis on internal descriptions of religious experience.

In disallowing (2) 'I saw God' but allowing (1) 'I see a table', Swinburne is already embarking on the wrong path. For strictly, on his own analysis of 'experience', (1) translates into:

(3) I have a mental experience (or percept) of seeming to see a table which causes the belief that I am seeing a table, and this belief is so strongly supported (I can have other similar perceptions of the table and others can have similar perceptions of the same table) that for practical purposes I can claim, 'I see the table'. Neither in principle nor in practice is there much difficulty in establishing the truth of (1).

Now (2) does not at all translate straightforwardly into:

(4) I had a mental experience of seeming to see God which caused the belief that I was seeing God, and this belief is so well established (I can get similar perceptions of God and others can

have like perceptions of God) that for practical purposes I can claim I saw God. One reason why (2) does not easily translate into (4) is that it is difficult to spell out what 'seeing God', as opposed to 'seeing a table', amounts to. Moreover one cannot say whether further perceptions of God would be at all similar to my first one nor does it seem that other persons can easily have perceptions of God. Perhaps these difficulties are not in principle insurmountable and that it is possible to offer an anaysis of 'I see God' much on the lines of 'I see a table'. Were this possible, it would appear to afford the best route from religious experience to the existence of God. But at the outset of his discussion Swinburne rules out this approach and concentrates rather on religious experience internally described, on the face of it a much more hazardous enterprise so far as establishing God's existence on the basis of religious experience is concerned. Swinburne concentrates on an analysis of the internal description of religious experience. Thus:

(5)   I had a mental experience of seeming to see (or hear; or it appeared, seemed to me that I saw or heard) God. Swinburne's discussion of statements of type (5) is not without its difficulties. Although he invokes the distinction between epistemic and non-epistemic or comparative uses of 'appears', 'seems', and 'looks', he fails to note that the non-epistemic use typically reports experience and the epistemic uses of these verbs have the function of reporting beliefs and opinions, not experiences.[19] Swinburne then concentrates on the epistemic uses of these words, and by appealing to a very wide interpretation of the principle of credulity, it is taken that a person's judging it to be the case that p is taken as evidence that p, irrespective of the basis of that person's judgment. On this very generous interpretation of the principle of credulity, that some objects in the sky appeared to be extra-terrestrial to some would be evidence that they were. This is clearly taking credulity too far!

In order to convince the reader of these criticisms, consider:
(6)   'The stick in water looks crooked to me.'
Here is an example of the non-epistemic use of 'looks'; it is used to report my mental experience of seeming to see a crooked stick in the water. But I do not *believe* the stick is bent. I believe it is straight for it was straight when I placed it in the water and I

hold the background belief that straight sticks appear crooked
when placed in water.
   Consider now:
   (7) 'The carpet looks red to me'.
This is the epistemic use of 'looks'. On the basis of a mental
experience of the carpet seeming to me to be red I report the
belief that it looks red. Now my having or experiencing the
mental experience is a good reason for *my* belief that the carpet
looks red, but it is not on its own sufficient for the truth of the
claim that the carpet is red. The truth of this latter claim is only
established if, among other things, others, viewing the carpet
from different positions under normal conditions of lighting,
report their belief that the carpet appears to be red. In short,
it is necessary to distinguish between reasonable grounds for the
belief that *p*, and reasonable grounds for the *truth* of *p*. Reasonable grounds for the belief that *p* cannot solely constitute reasonable grounds for the truth of *p*. I may have good reasons for
supposing that Jones believes his wife is out shopping, but
Jones's belief that his wife is out shopping does not of itself
establish the truth of the claim that his wife is out shopping.
That 'Jones believes that *p*' may be true and '*p*' false. The
conclusion of this discussion seems to be that we must reject
Swinburne's strong claim, based on a very wide application of
the principle of credulity, that,

> in the absence of special considerations, all religious experiences
> ought to be taken by their subjects as genuine, and hence as
> substantial grounds for belief in the existence of their apparent
> object — God, or Mary or Ultimate Reality or Poseidon.[20]

Having suggested that Swinburne's discussion of religious experience is largely misguided, resting as it appears to do on a
failure to appreciate fully the difference between the epistemic
and non-epistemic uses of 'appear', 'seems', 'looks', and because
it fails to give sufficient weight to the distinction between
reasonable grounds for X's belief that *p*, and reasonable
grounds for the truth of *p*, it must be granted that his discussion
raises at least two interesting points.
   Consider firstly:
   (8) 'I seemed to hear God'.
If the 'seeming' in (8) is taken, not as epistemic as with Swinburne, but as non-epistemic, the interesting question can be

raised whether one can have an experience of God, internally described in non-epistemic terms, as one can have an experience of seeming to see a crooked stick in the water, described in non-epistemic terms. Clearly such an experience of God requires a prior conception of what such a God is or would be like, and a major difficulty lies in providing such a conception. Consider, secondly, Swinburne's distinction between public and private perceptions. Thus a public perception can, following Swinburne, be formulated thus:

(9)   S perceives X (believing that he is doing so) if and only if an experience of its seeming (epistemically) to S that X is present is caused by X's being present, and X is such that as to cause all persons rightly positioned, with certain sense-organs and certain concepts, to pay a certain degree of attention, to have the experience of it seeming to them that X is present.

However, there may be an object O which causes certain persons to have the experience of its seeming to them that O is present without having that effect on all other attentive persons who occupy similar positions and have similar sense-organs and concepts.[21] If this condition is satisfied then S's perception of O is a private perception.

Clearly this distinction between private and public perceptions is perfectly acceptable. There are probably many cases in experience of music and the arts, for example, in which some persons have perceptions of objects O which are not perceived by others possessing normal sense-organs and concepts who are similarly placed. And granted that only a few claim to have had religious experiences, this might be the line one would, a priori, have expected Swinburne to follow. For example, even in the realm of visual perceptions, there may be reports of perceived experiences, epistemically described, which by the nature of the case cannot be experiences which the vast majority of people can have, and yet the reports have claims to be accepted as veridical. Consider the two successful climbers who reached the summit of Everest. On return they report that they had seen an abominable snowman, giving a description of what they had seen. Assuming the abominable snowman is a creature who only inhabits the higher reaches of the Himalayas, then the vast majority are never going to be in a position to have possible perceptions of this creature. The two climbers report that they had an experience of it seeming to them that they saw an abominable snowman. If the snowman was present, their report is true. But by the nature of the example very few of those to whom the report is made can be in a position to verify the claim. At this point we can invoke Swinburne's principle of credulity. We can accept the Everest climbers' report as prima-facie evidence for the existence of the snowman but not as conclusive evidence. That the climbers have a reputation for truthfulness and reliability, that it is very unlikely they were at the time under the infuence of drugs or suffering the adverse effects of high altitude, are all factors increasing the probability that they truly report what they report.

It seems to me that an argument from religious experience might well take this form, i.e. an attempt to establish that there are genuine private (in Swinburne's sense of private) religious perceptions. But it should be noted that the distinction between private and public perceptions is one within what Swinburne has called 'external descriptions' of religious experiences. Swinburne's strategy has been rather to concentrate on 'internal descriptions' of religious experiences, and so the approach suggested here of concentrating on private perceptions was not available to him.

1 Published London, Allen & Unwin, 1959.
2 Stephen R.L. Clark, *The Mysteries of Religion, An Introduction to Philosophy through Religion*, Oxford, Blackwell, 1986, p.215. It would be unfair to suggest that Professor Clark offers this as a 'definition' of religious experience: it is a statement of what religious experience is for most people. I am grateful to Professor T. McPherson for drawing my attention to this point.
3 Ibid., p.215.
4 It should be noted that on pages 217–20 Clark does discuss another aspect of religious experience, namely the 'interesting and immediate puzzle provided by solitary religious experience as distinguished from public ritual'.
5 Ibid., p.216.
6 Ibid.
7 H.H. Price, *Belief*, London, Allen & Unwin, 1969, p.455.
8 Ibid., p.471.

9 Ibid., p.474.
10 Ibid., p.475.
11 Ibid., pp.472–3.
12 Richard Swinburne, *The Existence of God*, Oxford, Clarendon Press, 1979, p.244.
13 Ibid., p.245.
14 Ibid., p.246.
15 Ibid., p.247.
16 Ibid., pp.247–8.
17 Ibid., p.248.
18 Ibid., p.254.
19 I am grateful to my colleage George Botterill for drawing my attention to this point.
20 Swinburne, op. cit., p.254.
21 Ibid., p.249.

The Issue of the Nature of Metaphysics

IVOR LECLERC

I

THE issue I wish to consider here — whether or not metaphysics is a valid enterprise — is still one which most prominently faces the philosophical community today, and most seriously divides it. I say 'still' because it has faced us for the last two centuries. This issue arose early in the nineteenth century as the outcome of the development of physics as a mechanics, that development which had initiated with Galileo and by the end of the seventeenth century had achieved a significant peak with Newton, and which reached its perfection by the end of the eighteenth century with Laplace.

Also with Laplace began a drive to disentangle the 'science of mechanics' from philosophy and from metaphysics in particular, by purging it of all of what were seen as relics of metaphysics surviving in such words as 'force', 'cause', 'law', 'energy', etc. — the last having been introduced at the beginning of the nineteenth century — by insisting on the admissibility of these terms in mechanics only as strictly quantitative concepts. That is, it was held to be necessary to extrude from these concepts not only all anthropomorphic presuppositions, but also all thought of the 'nature of' and 'sources of'. 'Force', for example, it was held had to be conceived solely as a quantitative ratio between mass and acceleration, and 'cause' conceived in terms of the mathematical notion of function.

This programme reached its full systematic development in the later part of the nineteenth century in the doctrine of Mach, Kirchhoff, and Hertz, Mach's *The Science of Mechanics* having been especially influential. The general success of the progamme was signified in the late nineteenth century by the use of the word 'science' as a synonym for 'natural or physical science', thereby proclaiming the full separation of physical science from philosophy.

The impact on philosophy of the triumph of the science of mechanics was variously manifested. Most important was the abandonment by philosophy, in the early nineteenth century, of the field of nature, philosophy thereby acquiescing in the claim of 'science' as the positive, that is, genuine, certain, true, knowledge of nature. Among philosophers this new 'positivist' conception of 'science' was propagated particularly by Auguste Comte (stimulated to this by the work of Lagrange) and by Avenarius (whose epistemological position was close to that of Mach). This line of thought was then extensively developed in the early twentieth century by groups of thinkers under various labels: the Vienna Circle, empirico-criticism, logical positivism, neo-positivism, analytical philosophy, and so on.

Although this positivist movement has been the one most vociferously anti-metaphysical and, by the spirit of intellectual intolerance which it engendered, has been the strongest influence toward the decline of metaphysics in this century, other significant influences in that direction should not be overlooked. Another most important manifestation of the effect on philosophy of the nineteenth-century developments in physical science was the turning of philosophy to epistemology as fundamental. This movement of thought, in which the influence of Kant and of Hume were prominent, has on the whole been decidedly anti-metaphysical, or at best not sympathetic to metaphysics.

One other most important effect on philosophy of the nineteenth-century developments in physical science was a reaction to it, one which stimulated metaphysics, engendering the flourishing of metaphysical schemes of the idealist variety. Then in the twentieth century the reaction to that idealist kind of metaphysics was for many the rejection of metaphysics entirely, and a capitulation to positivism.

Throughout the last two centuries the influence of natural science on philosophy has therefore been profound, and it will continue to be so in future, for reasons which will be clear as we proceed.

Especially pertinent to us in our time are the truly revolutionary advances in the natural sciences which have occurred in the last hundred years. Despite these the positivist doctrine of Mach has remained strong among, and indeed the orthodoxy of, the majority of scientists, inhibiting, and indeed preventing, the realization that those advances had rendered the theory of mechanism untenable as a fundamental conception of the nature of the physical. Those advances also entail the complete demolition of the positivist doctrine. However, the appreciation that this is the case has continued to be prevented by the persistence of the positivist attitude of mind to which so very many philosophers in this century have fallen prey.

The situation we are in today is that the twentieth-century developments in the natural sciences have effected a revolutionary change in thought of a magnitude at least of that of the seventeenth century. What has been most profoundly affected is, in the first place, the very conception of this science, not only in respect of its being fundamentally a mechanics but, of quite equal importance, of its being an autonomous discipline, independent of philosophy and especially of metaphysics.

In the second place what has been affected is the conception of philosophy, and in particular that of metaphysics, not only in that the entire positivist conception of philosophy has been rendered inapposite, but in that those developments in the natural sciences have made metaphysics essential to the inquiry into nature.

II

This has made acute the problem of the nature of metaphysics. For this is not adequately to be understood by a recurrence to, for example, the idealist metaphysics of the nineteenth century, with its fundamental categories those of spirit or mind. I would submit that today there is no adequate alternative, for achieving this understanding, to a systematic inquiry into metaphysical thought from its beginnings. It will not suffice, however, to pursue this inquiry in abstraction from the role of metaphysics in the total philosophical endeavour.

One evident line in the pursuit of this inquiry is to examine

how the enterprise has been conceived by great thinkers in the
past. For this we need to start with Aristotle, for he was the first
to define the field. The term 'metaphysics' itself did not actually
originate with him; it came into use somewhat later, not simply
as a title for the set of treatises which still bears that name, as
has been so frequently supposed, but as characterizing Aristotle's own view of that field — which he himself referred to as *prote
philosophia*, 'primary philosophy' — namely the set of issues and
problems which are arrived at *meta*, 'after' the study of the
physical, arising out of that study, but going 'beyond' the
physical. This field extends beyond that of the physical in not
being concerned, as is the physical inquiry, with particular
kinds of things, but deals with all beings (*ta onta*), that is, all
things which are, but with them '*qua* beings' (*he onta*)[1]; that is,
it considers being universally (*katholou*) *qua* being (*he on*).[2]

The word 'being' (*to on*), however, as Aristotle frequently
points out, is used in many senses, for not only the singular
things 'are', but also qualities, quantities, etc., also 'are', though
in a different sense, since they, in contrast to the singular things,
are not self-subsistent.[3] Thus of these senses, that of the self-
subsistent 'being' — which Aristotle termed *ousia* — must be
primary, and therefore 'it will be of *ousia* that the philosopher
must grasp the principles and causes'.[4]

In these last words, namely 'principles and causes', we have
another characterization by Aristotle of metaphysics, that is, as
the science of first principles and causes. The connection with
the former characterization, namely, of metaphysics as the
science of being *qua* being, is that 'since we are seeking the first
principles and highest causes (*de tas archas kai tas akrotatas aitias*),
clearly there must be some thing to which these belong by
virtue of its own nature[5], namely as *ousia*. These principles and
causes are *katholou*, 'universal', for they pertain not to any
particular kind or class of beings, but universally to all beings,
all *ousiai*.

Thus we have two designations of metaphysics, as the science
(*episteme*) of first principles and causes, and as the science of
'being *qua* being' (*to on he on*). Since the principles and causes are
those of being, it is being which is primary. Aristotle elucidated
this primacy in Chapter 1 of *Metaphysics*, Book Zeta:

> the question which has been raised of old and is raised now and
> always, and is always the subject of doubt (*aporoumenon*), viz.

what being is (*ti to on*), is just the question, what is *ousia* (*tis he ousia*). For it is this which some assert to be one, others more than one, and that some assert to be limited in number, others unlimited. And so we must consider chiefly and primarily and almost exclusively what that is which *is* in *this* sense.[6]

In the Hellenistic period, and indeed among Aristotle's immediate followers, the basic emphasis was put on the *ousia* which was held to be primary, namely the divine — this having some textual ground in Aristotle himself— and this became the determinative position of thinkers who had, in the first centuries of the Christian era, absorbed Greek philosophy as the foundation of their theology. That is, with this answer to the question of 'what is that which *is* in *this* sense', metaphysics essentially became theology — i.e. the 'object' of metaphysics was God. It is most important in the systematic inquiry into metaphysics to pursue an examination of this through the long Middle Ages. This, however, is not the occasion to do so. It will suffice for now to observe that this had involved giving a restrictive interpretation to the '*meta*' in 'metaphysics', one which, it seems to me, is not in accord with Aristotle's doctrine.[7] Relevant here is that it was particularly this interpretation which in the eighteenth century came to be rejected. In this rejection, however, the baby was thrown out with the bathwater: metaphysics was rejected along with theology, as fundamentally relevant to the inquiry into the physical.

I would suggest that what is necessary today is to return to a consideration and examination of metaphysics as the inquiry into the issues and problems which are involved in the inquiry into the physical, but which extend 'beyond' that inquiry, in the sense of not themselves being included in the subject matter or object of the physical inquiry.

III

For the comprehension of these issues it will be best to turn to a consideration of that crucial development in the seventeenth century, effectively initiated by Galileo, of the inquiry into the physical as a mechanics, that is, as a mathematical investigation of bodies in motion, that which had become so triumphantly successful. For most thinkers that success was alone sufficient to gain its overwhelming acceptance as 'science', the positive, certain, knowledge. But in the seventeenth century among some philosophers the question arose as to what was entailed in that conception of the inquiry into the physical as a mechanics. First there was the question as to why it should be that *mathematics* should provide the truth about the physical. This is a question, an issue, which goes 'beyond' mechanics — it is not an issue which occurs within mechanics, and which cannot be resolved mathematically, being rather presupposed by mechanics. Galileo himself saw it as an issue, to which his answer was that the world had been created by God as a mathematical structure, an answer which was accepted also by Descartes, Leibniz, Newton, and indeed virtually all at that time who were involved in the new development of thought. With the elimination, after the eighteenth century, of that portion of the answer about God's having created the world, this answer, namely, that the world is a mathematical structure, has remained the tacit metaphysical presupposition of the inquiry into the physical down to the present day. This is a metaphysical doctrine, and it requires to be justified — a mere pragmatical justification is insufficient.

Descartes was the first to see that there was, however, more involved than that, namely an entirely new conception of the physical *per se*. This new conception had been most explicitly formulated by Descartes' older compatriot, Sebastian Basso — though there were a number who were at the time thinking along the same lines. This new conception was of the physical as *matter*. This again is a conception which has persisted down to the present day. But to Descartes it was clear that this raised the philosophical, i.e. metaphysical, issue of what is 'matter', of what precisely is meant by that term; its meaning could not be taken as being self-evident.

Descartes saw that what was entailed is that matter 'is', that matter is that which ultimately 'is', i.e. which is physical 'being'. In other words, here was the seventeenth-century answer to Aristotle's question of 'what that is which *is* in *this* sense', the sense of *ousia* — which medieval thought had come to render by *substantia*, 'substance'. Descartes' definition of 'substance' was: 'By *"substance"*, we can understand nothing other than a thing which exists in such a way that it needs no other thing in order to exist'.[8] This is his rendering of Aristotle's conception of *ousia* as 'individual' (*to kath hekaston*),[9] as a self-subsisting being. But more was entailed in 'matter' than that it is individual, self-susbsisting being or substance.

This new doctrine of matter as being or substance entailed the rejection of the Aristotelian doctrine of physical being as analysable into, as composite of, matter and form. In the new doctrine, matter alone constituted physical being. But it entailed something further. The reason why in this new doctrine physical being was held to be matter to the exclusion of form was that in the antecedent period form had been the principle of change, of *motus*, in the physical, which meant that the physical in itself involved change — this had indeed been the fundamental Greek conception of the physical — and the new conception was that the physical is in itself immutable, no physical thing changing into another physical thing. Now 'matter' was that which had, from the introduction of the concept by Aristotle, been seen to be in itself changeless. Further, what was operative here was that the anti-Aristotelian conception of being, namely that of Neoplatonism, was of 'being' as in itself changeless, immutable. Thus it had been concluded that since matter is immutable, and since being is immutable, matter must be being, physical being. This evidently entailed, as Descartes was the first clearly to see, a metaphysical dualism, i.e. two different and mutually exclusive kinds of being, a physical being and a psychical being. This again is a metaphysical doctrine which has persisted down to the present day, more particularly among 'scientists', but also among the great majority of contemporary philosophers.

But in this century the issue of being has again come crucially to the fore, as the outcome of developments in physical theory. For these have made the conception of matter as immutable being untenable. The positivistic attempt to eliminate from physical theory the concepts of 'force', 'cause', 'energy', etc., except as quantititive ratios or magnitudes, has broken down. In contemporary physical theory physical entities have come to be thought of as centres of 'force' and 'activity', that is the very opposite of being in themselves changeless. Moreover, it has been found that there is a vast number of different kinds of what seem to be the ultimate, incomposite entities, and indeed that some seem capable of changing into other kinds.

What is entailed is that today a whole range of fundamental issues has risen, issues which are involved in, but which are yet *meta*, beyond, physical theory itself. Physical scientists themselves have on the whole had relatively scant appreciation of this because the heritage of a realization of issues as being *meta*, beyond, the physical has been lost in the last two centuries. Indeed even the philosophical tradition has suffered that loss, which is why metaphysics today has become doubly of crucial importance, namely to come to an adequate understanding of what metaphysics as a discipline or science is, and to make this available to thinkers in the other sciences.

IV

I would submit that if metaphysics in our time is to become again a really viable enterprise, then it is necessary to understand its nature as fundamentally a 'meta-physics', that is, a going beyond physics, which means approaching it from physics — i.e. the inquiry into nature in all its branches — to what is general or universal (*katholou*), as involved in the physical, but which transcends the inquiry into the physical as not itself being that which is the object in physical inquiry, since it is what is presupposed in physical inquiry. This means that it is not sufficient to approach the metaphysical enterprise by taking it, in complete abstraction, as the inquiry into being *qua* being, or the inquiry into first principles and causes. Because such an approach is too abstract it is all too liable to lead to schemes which are out of contact with vast areas of what is, especially the area of nature — examples of this are legion.

On the other hand, when the meta-physical issues are approached from the physical, especially in the present context of thought in the natural sciences, it will be found that it is indeed the issue of being which comes to the fore with singular pertinence. For example, in physical inquiry in this century many micro entities have been discovered of which there had previously been no inkling; that is to say, there 'are' electrons, protons, positrons, neutrons, neutrinos, photons, etc., most of which are spoken of as 'elementary', i.e. not composite, but the constituents of composites — though some of them are now suspected of in fact being composite, composed of quarks. There also 'are' the composite entities, atoms, molecules and, in the biological field, cells, of a very great variety of kinds. Further, in the biological field are still larger composites, vegetative and animal. But it cannot be maintained that they all 'are' in a sense different from that in which the elements 'are', since atoms, etc. 'are' as being composite, i.e. they 'are' as pluralities, which is quite different from the respect in which the elements 'are'.

But this raises the issue of whether the sense in which composites, such as atoms, molecules, and cells, 'are' is simply that of an aggregate collection, a heap? It is evident in contemporary physical theory that this is not the case, that on the contrary they are structured units, which is to say that they 'are' by virtue of their particular structure — which includes a structured interactivity of the constituent entities. In other words, their 'being' is a function of their structure, and not simply of their compositeness — this is particularly clear in chemistry and biology. Now this entails the metaphysical conclusion that their 'being' is not reducible to the being of the constituents. That is, the elementary constituents do not have 'being' in a 'primary' sense, from which that of the composites is 'derivative'. One outcome of this metaphysical consideration is the untenability of the prevailing orthodoxy in the natural sciences that biology is reducible to chemistry, and that chemistry is reducible to physics.

I have been concerned here to show how a central metaphysical issue, that of being, arises in the context of physical science. But even then it is not satisfactory to proceed to the metaphysical inquiry into being abstractly, in disconnection from the physical inquiry. Rather, the metaphysical inquiry must proceed with the physical inquiry as its background, as it had been for Aristotle, and also for Descartes and others in the seventeenth century. That is, it is the physical inquiry which evidences the requirement for a general or universal concept of 'being'. Now there is no valid logical process of induction to this general concept, any more than there is to, for example, 'natural laws'. The procedure can be, and to some extent has to be, by a speculative generalization, what has sometimes been called 'inductive generalization'. However, here, as in physical inquiry, the general concept arrived at is necessarily hypothetical — the claim to absolutely certain, 'clear and distinct', ultimate truths from which metaphysical reasoning can proceed deductively, is unacceptable; what Descartes and many others had supposed to be such truths are evidently hypotheses held with great conviction. All metaphysical hypotheses require rigorous examination, in respect of their internal coherence and consistency, and also with regard to their coherence and consistency with the theory and findings of the natural sciences. That is, in metaphysics the procedure is hypothetico-deductive, as it has now come widely to be appreciated as pertaining in the natural sciences.

Time does not permit my going further into the problems and procedure of metaphysics as a discipline. I should like in conclusion to make one further point in respect of the relation of philosophy, and of metaphysics in particular, to natural science. Physical or natural science has today broken down the comfortable haven of philosophy constituted by the acceptance, explicit or implicit, of the dualism dominant since the seventeenth century. For with the contemporary inquiries in, for example, physical chemistry, microbiology, and neurology, that dualism has ceased to be effective, for the problems of the nature of life and of mind or soul have entered the arena of attention of the natural scientists. The stage has passed in which natural scientists have been concerned merely with the problems of the mechanism and physical structure of living processes, and with the physical neurological processes. Indeed, 'life' itself, and 'mentality' itself, have become intrinsically relevant to the inquiry in these natural sciences. But the inquiry in these fields is being seriously hampered because, in the absence of the realization of issues as *meta* (beyond) those of physical inquiry *per se*, the natural scientists continue pursuing their inquiries in terms of the presuppositions of the material, mechanistic metaphysics of the antecedent epoch, with the result that 'life' and 'mind' are interpreted in terms of physical processes, and thereby what is essential to their physical inquiries is lost to them.

But this intrinsic relevance of 'life' and 'mind' to the inquiries into the physical processes is something which is of vital import to philosophers too, for 'mind' particularly had been accepted since the eighteenth century as the peculiar prerogative of philosophy, and now it must be recognized that mind is not as ontologically separate from the physical as has continued to be presupposed. This faces philosophy with the necessity of a fundamental rethinking of the entire issue of 'mind', and in this reassessment it is indispensable that the findings of the natural sciences be fully taken into account. Not to do so entails continuing in the presuppositions of dualism, with the consequence of philosophy being unable to contribute what is crucially requisite to the inquiries in natural science.

For what has come to be necessary today is an effective partnership of the natural sciences and metaphysics, since not only is neither of these as autonomous as has been believed for the last two centuries, but they are also mutually necessary to each other.

1 Aristotle, *Metaphysics*, 1003b15–16. (See *The Works of Aristotle*, Vol. VIII, Oxford, Clarendon Press, 1960).
2 Ibid., 1003a23–5.
3 Ibid., cf 1003b6–10.
4 Ibid., 1003b17–18.
5 Ibid., 1003a27–8.
6 Ibid., 1028a31–1028b6.
7 I have dealt with this at length in a forthcoming book, *The Metaphysical Foundations of Natural Science*.
8 Descartes, *Principles of Philosophy*, I, 51, trans. V.R. and R.P. Miller, Reidel, 1983.
9 Aristotle, *Metaphysics*, 1001a.

The Soul and Person, in Theological Perspective

T.F. TORRANCE

I

IN the early centuries of our era when the foundations of classical Christian theology were being laid, the doctrines of the Creation and Incarnation had a decisive impact upon the understanding of *soul* and *person*. Belief in the transcendent God who had created the universe out of nothing and endowed it with a created rational order of its own, called into question Greek philosophical notions of a separation between the intelligible and sensible realms, or between form and matter, and all attendant ideas about the timeless divine nature of rational forms immanent in the world and the ultimate unreality and irrationality of sensible or material phenomena. With Christian theology, matter and form, sensible and intelligible realities, were regarded as equally created out of nothing and as inseparably unified in one contingent rational order pervading the whole universe of visible and invisible realities including the body and mind of human being. The decisive factor, however, was the doctrine of the Incarnation through which the doctrine of creation out of nothing, which Christians shared with Jews, was radicalized. On the one hand, the doctrine of the Incarnation of the Word or Logos of God within the structures of the physical world had the effect of overthrowing the Greek idea of the Logos as an immanent cosmological principle, and demanded a sharp distinction between the uncreated rationality of God and the created rationalities of the cosmos. At the same time it insisted on the full reality of matter and the rationality of contingent existence. On the other hand, the doctrine that in Jesus Christ God's own eternal Logos had personally become man within space and time shattered all forms of cosmological dualism, whether Platonic, Aristotelian or Stoic, which did not allow for any interaction of God with the empirical world. It undermined the impersonal or merely quasi-personal modes of thought that had characterized Hellenic religion, philosophy and culture, and gave rise to the distinctive category of the *person* which had hitherto not been reached even within the Hebraic world of thought.

Within the Greek world of thought, which identified the real with the immutably and timelessly true and discounted the realm of changing empirical events as deficient in rationality, scientific knowledge was inevitably restricted to the realm of necessary truths of reason and changeless geometrical and logical forms detached from space and time. A genuine empirical science in our sense could not have arisen until the controlling axiomatic structure of Greek dualism and the fundamental combination of ideas it involved were overthrown. That is what began to take place through the Christian view of God and his relation to the world, although the new theological understanding of the contingent nature and order of the universe had to struggle for many centuries with deeply in-built habits of thought deriving from classical antiquity before it could bear fruit in the actual emergence of natural science.

Early in that development, belief that the Word of God by whom all things are made had himself become *Man* within the creation had profound implications for the understanding of man in his relation to God on the one hand and in his relation to contingent reality on the other hand. Thus there arose a distinctive Christian anthropology in accordance with which man is given a unique place in the creative and providential purpose of God for the universe, as the creature who exists as a spiritual and physical being on the boundary between heaven and earth, eternity and time, grace and nature, the creature with whose destiny the whole created order is bound up. This Judaeo-Christian understanding of human being and nature inevitably clashed with the dualist conceptions of man that prevailed in Graeco-Roman religion and society, but the Church also took over some current terms from Middle-Platonism and recast them in the service of its own theological articulation in forms that have left their mark upon subsequent developments. It is by way of reflection on the notions of *soul* and *person* that emerged out of this early patristic anthropology that this brief essay is offered.

II

The Soul

In the dualist outlook of Greek religion and philosophy, the soul was regarded as intrinsically divine and immortal but temporarily imprisoned in a body where it is entangled in the darkness and irrationality of matter and corruption. In contrast, Christian theology, in line with the Hebraic tradition, developed a unitary view of human being, in which soul (including mind) and body, instead of being regarded as antithetical, were regarded as essentially complementary and ontologically integrated. As created by God, man is indivisibly *body of his soul and soul of his body*, yet in such a way that, as Athanasius expressed it, his soul endowed with mind (*nous*) has primacy over his body.[1] It is as this living whole that man is addressed by the Word of God and made to reflect him (*ad imaginem Dei*) in a unique relation which transcends his creatureliness and is constitutive of his distinctively *human* being and nature as a 'rational animal' who is capable of thinking of what is outside of and beyond himself.[2] The soul itself, however, like the body, is brought into being out of nothing, and as a creature is inherently transient and liable to dissolve back into nothing, for it has no inherent force perpetuating its existence. Like all created things it is corruptible, and may disintegrate and cease to exist. Nevertheless, it is continuously sustained in its existence by the beneficent will and creative presence of God, and is thus given immortality through the grace of a relation with God who only has immortality.[3] God alone is uncreated, perfectly self-sufficient Being, eternally existing in himself in an utterly transcendent way that surpasses our power to comprehend. He is without beginning and without end; to be immortal is the natural or intrinsic property of his Being. All other being is intrinsically deficient in existence and naturally mortal with a finite beginning and a finite end, and is thus completely dependent on the goodness of God, the Lord of all being, in the order of its existence. So far as man is concerned, however, owing to the distinctive integration of his soul and body, a continuing personal life after death has to include the body as a basic equation of existence. Hence in Christian theology immortality is inseparably bound up with the resurrection of the whole being of man as body of his soul and soul of his body, and is described as a creaturely participation in the uncreated eternal Life of God.[4]

It is in the resurrection that the full purpose of God in the creation of human being for communion with himself is brought to its fruition. In the teaching of the New Testament the resurrection is certainly a redemptive act completing the atoning and saving work of God in the life and death of Jesus Christ, in delivering man from the corruption that had come to afflict his creaturely existence. It is also an ontological act, restoring true creaturehood to man by establishing it in an intimate relation to the creative Source of all being. As such the resurrection recapitulates and transcends the original creation of man, making good the deficiency in the unstable, fleeting nature of his contingent being, and finalizing his reality and integrity as body of his soul and soul of his body through giving him participation in the eternal life of God embodied in his Incarnate Son.

It is understandable, therefore, that the Church Apologists of the second century quickly pointed to the Resurrection of Jesus Christ in the wholeness of his human being in justification of Christian teaching that the whole man composed of soul and body, though created by the Word of God out of nothing, does not cease with death but is called to life and resurrection.[5] Against attacks, particularly by Platonists, they insisted that in creation God did not give being and life either to the soul by itself or to the body by itself, but to *man* in whom body and soul form a single living entity. Moreover, it is *man* not the soul by itself, who is endowed with intellect and reason, and *man* who survives death, although only through resurrection. Thus it was claimed that apart from the resurrection, and its inner link with the purpose of God in creation, man could not survive as man. In what the resurrection has to say about the fact and the nature of the continuity of human life beyond death, however, it tells us what man really *is* as man. He is man made by God to be in living communion with himself, the creative Source of Life, and may not therefore cease to be what he is meant by God to be as man in the wholeness of his human being and nature.

The resurrection of man in soul and body to which the Apologists pointed, of course, was that which we experience through union with Jesus Christ, for it is his resurrection from the dead that is the generating source and ground of our resurrection. The inner ontological connection between our resurrection and that of Christ began to be thought out by Irenaeus in the second century, but it was only with theologians like Athanasius and Hilary after the Christological developments of the fourth century that it became clarified.

Two cognate points may be noted, for they bear on our theme. First, the astonishing oneness of Creator and creature involved in the Incarnation was understood to indicate not only what God purposed to happen to man in his creation but what God has now actually established as the permanent foundation on which creaturely human being is secured in nature and existence against the menace of nothingness constantly hanging over it, the threat of what the Greeks called *me on*. Essentially contingent though man's creaturely being is, it has now been anchored in the irrefragable oneness of Creator and creature in the Incarnate Word, and may not therefore cease to be what it is in Jesus Christ. Second, the assuming by the Incarnate Son of God of our estranged human nature into himself in inseparable union with his divine nature has the effect of healing our nature of its depravity and saving it from eventual dissolution. Instead of succumbing to corruption in the grave and the disintegration of body and soul in death, Jesus rose again in the fullness and wholeness of his human being, thereby resurrecting human nature in himself in the identity and integrity of man as body of his soul and soul of his body. Thus the Christian Church held that in the Incarnation and Resurrection of Christ there took place the affirmation and finalizing of man's creation, the establishing of his creaturely human reality in a wholeness that does not crumble away into dust or degenerate into nothingness, but continues in a living relation with God the Father Almighty, Maker of all things visible and invisible. Thus the Incarnation and Resurrection were regarded as establishing the distinctively Christian view of man as an integrated whole, not as soul and body, but as 'embodied soul and besouled body'.[6]

This doctrine of the unity of soul and body was discerned to have two far-reaching implications which are not without their relevance for us today.

(1) The inseparability of soul and body had to apply to the human embryo from the moment of its conception. Although the distinctive features of human being are not yet visible in any differentiated form, the essential nature of the embryo is nevertheless to be regarded as that of a living human being which as such is the object of God's concern as much as a child or an adult.[7] There can be little doubt that this view was considerably influenced by the New Testament teaching that the human life of Jesus commenced from the moment of his conception by the Holy Spirit in the womb of the Virgin Mary. It was thus that the Early Church felt obliged to reject abortion and feticide as well as infanticide.[8]

The fullest consideration of the beginning of human existence in the light of the conjunction of the soul and body, was offered by Gregory of Nyssa. He argued that since man's being is one, consisting of soul and body, the beginning of his existence must be one as well: soul and body come into being at the same moment on the occasion of generation.[9] In line with other leading Greek theologians[10] Gregory held that each soul, far from being pre-existent as Platonists and Origenists held, is created by God along with the body and grows together with the body from the moment of its conception. Thus as the form of the future man is potentially present from the beginning although it is as yet concealed, so the human soul must be regarded as invisibly present at every stage in the development of the embryo, but as becoming increasingly 'manifest' through its own proper and natural operation, as it advances concurrently with the growth of the body. This idea that the human being is already potentially complete in 'the human germ' as Gregory expressed it, is startlingly similar to the modern scientific finding that the human being is genetically complete in the embryo from the moment of its conception, which makes abortion or feticide as morally and utterly abhorrent as infanticide.

(2) The ontological inseparability of soul and body in the human being applies to the distinction between male and female. It means that difference in sex is not simply a feature of the body, merely adventitious or accidental to the soul, but is intrinsic to the human soul which, far from being neutral, *is*

either male or female. The full implication of the unity of soul and body in the human being in this respect was not realized in patristic theology, owing to the generally accepted biological idea that it is in the male sperm alone that the whole 'seed' of human being is contained, with the female supplying only the womb to shelter its germination and nourish its growth into infancy. On the other hand, the Biblical teaching about the 'goodness' of what God had created, together with its rejection of dualist and Manichaeistic denigration of the body as evil, gave rise to a more positive evaluation of sexual difference as constitutive of human nature. Sexuality thus determines the innermost being of people, making them either male or female in themselves.

However, in that the basic form of humanity, or the essential human nucleus, is neither man by himself nor woman by herself, but only man and woman, man *is* man only in relation to woman, and woman *is* woman only in relation to man. This was in accord with the teaching of Jesus about marriage, that man and woman are not finally two but one, and that this difference with the oneness and fullness of human being, far from being an external convention, is to be traced back to a conjunction between man and woman in God's original creation which must not be put asunder. It should be pointed out that this divinely instituted union between man and woman is a characteristic not only of their creation but of their life in the resurrection in which their creation as man and woman will be brought to its ultimate completion. Certainly, as Jesus said, in the resurrection people neither marry nor are given in marriage, for life in the resurrection transcends the kind of temporal processes we experience in this world, but the bond of union between man and woman remains intact — far from being dissolved by the resurrection, it will be perfected and eternalized.

Embedded in the otherness and togetherness of man and woman in love and marriage, each of whom is an independent and distinctive human being in partnership with the other, there is an inherent relatedness in human being which is a creaturely reflection of a transcendent relatedness in divine Being. This is the *personal* or *inter-personal* structure of humanity in which there is imaged the ineffable personal relations of the

Holy Trinity. St Augustine once put his finger on the point
when he wrote: 'While the image of the Trinity is one person,
the Supreme Trinity himself is three Persons.'[11] However, it is
not the individual person that we are now to consider, but the
person in ontological relation with other persons.[12]

III

The Person

In general, Greek patristic anthropology, as we have seen,
thought of man in a non-dualist biblical way as a unitary being
whose body is the body of his soul and whose soul is the soul of
his body. It gave little place to a trichotomist account of man
in terms of body, soul and mind, for it preferred to think of the
whole being of man as endowed with intelligence and reason.
Likewise it gave little place to a psychological analysis of man
as comprising body, soul and spirit, but preferred to think of
man in body and soul as related to God through the power and
presence of his Spirit, and thereby endowed with the capacity
to think and act in accordance with the nature (*kata physin*) of
what is other than himself. In this view the human 'spirit' is
essentially a dynamic correlate of the divine 'Spirit'. It refers,
not to a third thing in man beside soul and body, but to a
transcendental determination of his existence in soul and body,
constituting him as a human being before God in relation to
other human beings. The 'spirit' of man, therefore, is not
something he possesses in himself as an ingredient or potency in
his make-up, or as a 'spark of the divine', but the ontological
qualification of his soul, and indeed of his whole creaturely
being, brought about and maintained by the Holy Spirit, in
virtue of which he lives and moves and has his being in God, as
man made in his image and likeness. It is, then, in virtue of this
transcendental determination of his being as embodied soul
that man is made capable of thinking objectively of what is
other than himself and of passing judgement about it — which
is, of course, the very essence of his human rationality.
  St Basil characterized this creative and life-giving activity of
the Spirit by distinguishing it as 'the perfecting cause' (*he*

teleiotike aitia) in relation to the work of the Father as 'the originating cause' (*he prokatarktike aitia*) and the work of the Son as 'the moulding cause' (*he demiourgike aitia*).[13] Although infinitely exalted above and beyond all creatures, the Spirit of God is nevertheless free to be present to the creature and as the perfecting cause to realize and bring to completion the creative purpose of God for the creature. He does this not only from the side of the Creator toward the creature but from the side of the creature toward the Creator by bringing its relations to their proper end (*telos*) in the Creator, and thereby establishing the creature in an enduring ontological relation to God. This means that, while the creature does not have any continuity in relation to God that belongs to the creature in itself, it does have a relation to God which is continuously given and unceasingly sustained by the presence of the Spirit. In every operation the Spirit is closely conjoined with, and inseparable from, the Father and the Son, for he is the Spirit of the Father and the Son. But a distinction is in order, and so Basil, following St Paul, spoke of the triune activity of God as *from* the Father, *through* the Son, and *in* the Spirit. Thus the special activity of the Spirit as Creator may be described as holding contingent reality *within* the embrace of his presence, thereby imparting to it the grace of continuance and consummating its relations with the ultimate source of its being and order in the Father and the Son.

Now the notion of *spirit* with which Basil operates here is intensely *personal* in the sharpest contrast to the impersonal notion of Hellenic religion and philosophy. This is the aspect of the doctrine of the Spirit that is prominent in Nicene theology, in its stress upon the transcendent Reality of the Holy Spirit as *Lord*, the sovereign divine *Subject* who speaks to us in the holy Scriptures and who is worshipped together with the Father and the Son. He is the personal Presence of God in the world, 'the living intelligent Principle' of all created being, who freely imparts life to the creature and sustains that life in himself within the embrace of his own uncreated Life.[14] It is in this way that we have to think of the creative and life-giving presence of the Holy Spirit to man. The Spirit of God the Father and the Son is God in his freedom personally to meet and be with man, to address him in his Word, making himself known to him and creating in him capacity to respond as a rational subject and agent to himself. It is through this inter-personal mode of his presence to man that the Spirit makes man's being open for fellowship with God, and thereby brings his creaturely relations to their true end and fulfilment in God. He is essentially the living Spirit who, coming from the inner Communion of the Holy Trinity, creates communion between man and God.

Undoubtedly the New Testament doctrine of the Holy Spirit, particularly as it was developed by Greek patristic theology, played a decisive role in the transition from an impersonal to a personal understanding of human being and of the operation of the human reason. A new approach to man's existence and nature set in, governed by a transcendental determination of man to an *objective other*, primarily in God but also in his fellow man, which turned the basic concept of man inside out. The Greek view of man as the embodiment of a divine soul, or of a soul as participating in the divine Reason, inevitably implied that man is turned in upon himself — hence the *gnothi seauton* of the Platonic Socrates — and that his reason functions under the control of innate preconceptions — hence the 'pugnacious proposition' of the *Meno*. That was the basic epistemological problem which, as Athanasius tells us, Christian theology met in its struggle with the Hellenizing modes of thought that erupted among Arian churchmen who operated with religious conceptions which they had devised and mythologically projected out of a centre in themselves into Deity.[15]

In Nicene theology, however, a profound epistemological inversion in the conception and function of the human reason took place on the basis of biblical teaching about the creation of man, in soul as well as body, out of nothing and about the indivisible unity of man as body and soul before God. With all animal being, man was held to be an organism comprising a body animated by a living soul, and like other animals to be inherently contingent and perishable. Unlike them he was a 'rational animal', which was due, not to a participation (*hethexis, metoche*) of his soul in divinity, but to the constitutive relation of man as body of his soul and soul of his body to God through his Spirit, which we have discussed. The Greek Fathers were deeply influenced by the teaching of Jesus that the Scripture 'called gods (*theoi*) those to whom the Word of God (*Logos*

Theou) came'.[16] While they spoke of this as *theosis* or *theopoiesis*, they meant by that, not a divinizing or deification of man's creaturely being but a distinctive transcendental determination of his being *for God* which both confirms it in its creaturely reality as utterly different from God and adapts man in his contingent nature for knowledge of God and fellowship with him. While the Holy Spirit was held to be the determining and integrating ground of man in the wholeness of his being as soul and body, they thought of the quickening and enlightening presence of the Spirit as bearing uniquely and directly upon man as soul of his body rather than as body of his soul, and in such a way as to give the soul priority or rule (*hegemonikon*) over his bodily existence. Thus for Greek patristic theology, the Holy Spirit is the dynamic Principle of man's existence and rationality in the wholeness of his being before God. It is in virtue of his being grasped and sustained by God's Spirit in this constitutive way that man may be said to be 'spirit' or to have 'spirit'.[17] While the spirit of man, as we have noted, is not to be regarded as an inherent feature of his being along with his soul and body, nevertheless it is owing to his being spirit or having spirit that man is sharply differentiated from all other animated bodies in the creation as rational being made *ad imaginem Dei*. In this event he may be understood not from an independent centre in himself but only from above and beyond himself in his transcendental relation to God.

It is not through any alleged participation in the essence of God, therefore, as Hellenic religion and philosophy maintained, but through the objective orientation of man in soul and body to God, the Source and Ground of all creaturely rationality and freedom, that man is constituted a rational subject and agent, i.e., a *person*. This takes place through the 'perfecting operation' (as St Basil called it) of the Holy Spirit in effecting meeting between man and God as subject to Subject, and therein adapting his creaturely being for communion with God. However, it is through the inner linking of this 'perfecting operation' of the Spirit with the 'moulding operation' of the Word of God by whom all things are made that the specifically personal nature of man's subject-being and the personal mode of his rationality arises. Hence through Jesus Christ, the Incarnate Son or Word of God, and in the Holy Spirit, it is possible for man to have direct access to God, to meet and know him personally, to hear him and speak to him face to face or person to person, and thus to experience in himself the transforming impact of God's personal Reality and Being.

It was certainly the new dimension of intimate knowledge and experience of God the Father mediated through the Son and in one Spirit that first gave rise to the notion of the personal, but it was only with the formulation of the doctrines of Christ and the Holy Trinity, in which the Church sought to give adequate expression to God's self-revelation to mankind in the Incarnation, that the technical theological concept of *person* was formed. The incarnate coming and presence (*ensarkos parousia*) of God in Jesus Christ had the effect of setting the relations between man and God on a decisively new basis, for it meant the acute personalization of God's interaction with mankind and indeed with all created reality. Hence, as Pringle-Pattison expressed it in his Gifford Lectures:

> The essential feature of the Christian conception of the world, in contrast to the Hellenic, may be said to be that it regards the person and the relations of persons to one another as the essence of reality.[18]

The technical term which Greek theology eventually adopted for 'person' was *hypostasis* which in current usage referred to self-subsistent being in its external objective relations in distinction to *ousia* which was used to refer to being in its interior relations. *Hypostasis*, however, was not taken over unchanged, but had to be adapted and charged for theological use.[19] Thus it was associated with *onoma* (name) and *prosopon* (face) to refer to what we know as self-identifying personal being or reality. This is evident above all in its application to the *Logos* who, far from being an impersonal cosmological principle, as we have seen, is God the Son, the *Autologos*, incarnate in Jesus Christ who reveals himself to us face to face and speaks to us directly in person (*ek prosopou*).[20] Under the transforming power of the Incarnation *hypostasis* became suitable to express the Church's understanding of the objective self-manifestation of God as Father, Son and Holy Spirit, that is, as three Persons (*hypostaseis*) in one Being (*Ousia*) — the regular formalization accepted for the Holy Trinity.[21] It was with the

Cappadocian and Alexandrian theologians particularly that the Christological and Trinitarian use and meaning of *hypostasis* became firmly established.[22]

It is highly significant that in its classical formulation the doctrine of the Trinity does not speak of three separated *hypostaseis* or Persons in God, but of Father, Son and Holy Spirit as three distinct Persons coinhering consubstantially in one another. That is to say, the Triune God is worshipped and adored as a transcendent Fullness of Personal Being, an ineffable Communion of Persons, in whom the Persons are who they are in their mutual or 'perichoretic' relations with one another in one and the same divine Being.[23] While *hypostasis* or *person* was used in this unique sense to speak of God as he is eternally in himself, it was also used in a secondary sense to speak of human persons who on their creaturely level exist only in such a way that the relations between them belong to what persons essentially are. Of course, human persons are not what they are in one and the same being, but, as we have seen, they are not without an inherent relatedness or 'community-ness' among themselves in which they bear a created reflection of the transcendent relatedness or 'community-ness' inherent in God. It is in virtue of this ontopersonal structure in humanity that human beings may rightly be understood as made in the image of God.

St Athanasius used to speak of Jesus, 'the Dominical Man' (*ho kyriakos anthropos*), as 'the Principle of ways' (*arche hodon*) which God has provided for us.[24] Whatever else that meant it pointed to the humanity which the Son of God had taken from us, healed in soul and body and sanctified or perfected through the Spirit in himself, as having archetypal significance for human beings. It is in Jesus himself that we discern what the basic structure of humanity is and ought to be, for in him we find the unity of soul and body, and the integration of the rational and the personal, which God the Father and Creator has purposed for each of us. Moreover, the realization that in Jesus Christ the human *mind* was not displaced by the divine Mind, but indivisibly united to it, had the effect of establishing the ontology of the creaturely human mind in an unprecedented way.[25] Hence it is to what took place in the incarnate life of the Word or Son of God, in the humanizing and personalizing of our human nature in Jesus himself and consequently in his humanizing and personalizing of others in their contact with him, that we are to look for insight into what the impact of God's personal Being must mean for us. It was thus that Cyril of Jerusalem spoke of the *enhypostatic* Being and Activity of both the Son and the Spirit in their healing and renewing impact upon the faithful.[26] Through Christ and in the Spirit there takes place an 'enhypostasizing' or personalizing of relations between man and God and correspondingly of relations between man and man.

In the strictest sense God alone is Person, for he is a fullness of personal Being, and as such is the creative Source of all other personal being. He is *Personalizing Person* whereas we are *personalized persons*. We are indebted to his creative activity and presence for our very existence, but we are also indebted to him for the personal mode of being which he unceasingly generates in us and among us through his Word and Spirit. It is through the Incarnation, however, that God interacts with us not only as God but as Man, and in such a way — this is the very heart of the Christian message — that he redeems us from our aliena-tion, reconciles us to himself and to one another in his divine love, and thus renews and confirms his personalizing deter-mination of our human being. Historically that is the source of the concept of *person* which has now become a universally recognized category of prime importance. Of course, once the concept of person was launched into the stream of human ideas, it was bound to develop an independent history of its own under the impact of different cultures and to move away from its original source. And that has happened, not always for the better, as is only too evident in the problematic idea of 'per-sonality' which is subjectively rather than objectively orien-tated, and seems inevitably to suffer from an in-built ambiguity if not a subtle hypocrisy.[27] It is, I believe, to Jesus himself, the Dominical Man, that we must constantly bring all our notions of human being, of soul and person, for healing and renewing.

---

1 Athanasius, *Contra Gentes*, 30–32; cf. Irenaeus, *Adversus haereses*, 5.6.1.
2 Thus Athanasius, op. cit, 31.

3 See my Drew Lecture on Immortality for 1980, reprinted in *Transformation and Convergence in the Frame of Knowledge*, Christian Journals Ltd,' Belfast, 1984, pp.333–49.
4 See the illuminating essays by Georges Florovsky on 'Creation and Creaturehood' and 'The "Immortality" of the Soul', *Creation and Redemption, Collected Works*, Vol. 3, Norland Publishing Company, Belmont, Mass., 1976, pp.43–78 and 213–40.
5 See especially Pseudo-Justin, *De resurrectione*, 1–10, *Bibliotheke Hellenon Pateron*, Vol. 4, Athens, 1955, pp.224–32; Athenagoras, *De resurrectione*, 13–25, *Bibliotheke Hellenon Pateron*, Vol. 4, Athens, 1955, pp.321–31.
6 This was Karl Barth's way of expressing it, *Christian Dogmatics*, III.2, T & T Clark, Edinburgh, pp. 325ff.
7 Athenagoras, *De resurrectione*, 17f and *Presbeia*, 35.6, *Bibliotheke Hellenon Pateron*, pp.26ff and 35f. cf. C. Stead, *Divine Substance*, Oxford University Press, 1977, p.229:

> Both Tertullian and Origen... express the view that the emission of human seed is of itself sufficient to release a fully individualized offspring in germinal form, which only needs shelter and nourishment in the womb.

8 See *The Didache of the Apostles*, 2.2 and *The Epistle of Barnabas*, 19.5: 'Thou shalt not procure abortion or commit infanticide'; likewise Athenagoras, *Presbeia*, 36.6; and Clement, *Paedagogos*, 2.96. Cf. also Philo, *De Specialibus legibus*, 3 and Josephus, *contra Apionem*, 2.
9 Gregory of Nyssa, *De anima et resurrectione*, MPG 46, 125–8; *De opificio hominis*, 28–9.
10 Gregory of Nazianzus, *Orationes*, 37.15: Cyril of Jerusalem, *Catecheses*, 4.18f; Epiphanius, *Anchoratus*, 55; Cyril of Alexandria, *In Johannem*, 1.9, etc.
11 Augustine, *De Trinitate*, 15.23.43.
12 The individualist conception of 'person' which came to prevail in Latin thought derives from Boethius, *De duabus naturis et una persona Christi, adversus Eutychen et Nestorium*, 2.1–5.
13 Basil, *De Spiritu Sancto*, 16.38; *Bibliotheke Hellenon Pateron*, Vol. 52, p.262.
14 This was the way in which Cyril of Jerusalem presented the teaching of the Church, *Catecheses*, 16–17.
15 This was the contrast which Athanasium drew between subjective thinking *kat'epinoian* and objective thinking *kata dianoian*, *De sententia Dionysii*, 2, 23f; *De synodis*, 15; *Contra Arianos*, 1.9, 37; 4.2.f; *Ad Episcopos Aegypti*, 12ff, etc.
16 St John, 10.35.
17 Cf. Karl Barth's enlightening exposition of this, *Church Dogmatics*, Eng. Tr, T & T Clark, Edinburgh, 1960, III.2, pp.344–66; and Ray S. Anderson, *On Being Human, Essays in Theological Anthropology*, William B. Eerdmans, Grand Rapids, Michigan, 1982, pp.207ff.
18 A. Seth Pringle-Pattison, *The Idea of God in the Light of Recent Philosophy*, Oxford University Press, 1920, p.291. Cf also the Gifford Lectures of C.C.J. Webb, *God and Personality*, Allen & Unwin, London, 1919.

19 I have given an account of this development in *Theology in Reconciliation*, Geoffrey Chapman, 1975, pp.243ff.
20 Athanasius, *Contra Gentes*, 40,46; *De Incarnatione*, 54; *Contra Arianos*, 4.2, etc.
21 Athanasius, *Expositio fidei*, 2; *In illud omnia*, 6; *Ad Antiochenos*, 6f.
22 See especially the statement of Gregory of Nyssa, attributed to his brother Basil as *Epistola* 38; and Cyril's second and third *Epistolae ad Nestorium*. Cf. Methodios Fouyas, *The Person of Jesus Christ in the Decisions of the Ecumenical Councils*, Central Printing Press, Addis Ababa, 1976, pp.53ff and 72ff.
23 For the *relational* nature of the divine hypostases see Gregory Nazianzen, *Orationes*, 29.16; 30.20; 31.8f; 40.41; 41.15.
24 Athanasius, *Expositio Fidei*, 1, 4.
25 Cf. the two works attributed to Athanasius known as *Contra Apollinarem*, I & II, *Bibliotheke Hellenon Pateron*, Vol. 37, pp.267–98.
26 Cyril of Jerusalem, *Catecheses*, 16.3; 17.5, 28, 33f.Cf. Athanasius, *Contra Apollinarem*, 1.20f. This idea was to be more fully developed by Cyril of Alexandria, Severus of Antioch and Leontius of Jerusalem.
27 Cf. T.E. Hulme's account of personality as a 'mixed' or 'bastard' thing, *Speculations*, Kegan Paul, London, 1936, pp.1, 25, 33, etc.

The Sinlessness of Jesus

H.P. OWEN

IN a long and distinguished career devoted to the study of philosophy and religion, Hywel Lewis has shown a marked interest in (among other subjects) ethics and Christology. I therefore hope that the topic I have chosen will be found appropriate.

From the beginning, Christians have believed that Christ was sinless. He was free both from original sin (that is, from evil impulses and inclinations) and from actual sin (that is, from evil acts freely committed, involving moral responsibility and requiring divine forgiveness). This belief is often stated and nowhere denied in the New Testament; it has strong conciliar support in the Chalcedonian Definition's statement that Christ was like us in all things except for sin; and it has been constantly affirmed by theologians (for example, by Schleiermacher in his *The Christian Faith*).[1] Furthermore, the belief has been continuously presupposed by the Church's liturgy and by individual devotion. Admittedly, the negative form of the belief is not sufficient. We must go on to affirm that Christ was perfect both spiritually and morally. Nevertheless, the negative form is the one that is usually discussed, and so it is the form that I shall consider.

Two basic questions arise. First, how do we know that Christ was sinless? It may be said that we know it through the gospels' record of his life. Certainly the evangelists give us the unqualified impression that Jesus was sinless. They never represent him as being conscious of sin. Rather they represent him as one who, although he mixed freely with sinners, felt himself to be so close to God that he could speak with divine authority in forgiving sins. He stands out clearly as the perfect exemplification of the commandments to love God and one's neighbour as oneself.[2] Yet the evidence of the gospels is defective in two respects. First, this evidence (though cogent and, so I should say, essential) is, at any rate for this purpose, not extensive. The evangelists do not give, and did not intend to give, a complete portrait of Jesus or a complete account of his words and acts. Secondly, it is doubtful whether any record of any person's life could strictly prove that he was sinless. No biographer could give an account of all his subject's words, deeds and (what supremely matters) states of mind.

In fact, the early Christians did not come to believe in Christ's sinlessness solely or even chiefly on the ground of his life and teaching. They came to believe in it through the redemptive impact that the risen Christ made on them by the operation of the Holy Spirit. In the risen Christ they experienced the total source of their salvation, an all-sufficient expiation for sin, the means of reconciliation to God, the fount of holiness, the author of a wholly new creation. I do not mean that Christians of the apostolic age inferred Christ's sinlessness from his saving work. Rather they apprehended it as inhering in the work., It was a matter of experience not inference. At the same time the logic of the apprehension can be unravelled in an inferential form. If Christ created a wholly new order of righteousness leading to life in exchange for an old order of sin leading to death, this can only be because he offered to God a sacrifice of perfect obedience and love. These Christians then found a confirmation of their experience in the record of Christ's earthly life.

It is important to put this apostolic experience of Christ in the context of the belief, grounded in the same experience, that as the risen Lord he merited an adoration due to God alone. In the view of the first Christians, Christ's saving work was not only a human one. It was also, in its own nature, divine and so stamped with the glory of God himself. The writers of the epistles and the fourth evangelist did not think of Jesus simply as a man whom God commissioned, by an influx of his Spirit, as a sinless agent of salvation. They thought of him as one who, while being wholly human, was also in his own person and in an entirely unique way divine, reflecting thus divine perfection. I shall consider belief in the Incarnation in dealing with the second question to which I now turn.

This is the question whether it was possible for Christ to sin.

Two views can be adopted here. According to the first (the weaker) view Christ might have sinned but in fact did not sin. According to the second (the stronger) view he could not have sinned (it was impossible for him to do so). It may be natural for some Christians to be impatient with this question as a typical example of theologians' tendency to raise questions that are irrelevant to faith and that are perhaps unanswerable. Surely, it may be said, it is enough to hold that Christ did not sin and that he was to that extent qualified to become our Redeemer. Although I sympathize with this reaction I do not think it is tenable. I suggest that this question, so far from being merely speculative, involves considerations of theological consistency and is clearly relevant to the ordinary believer's conception of Christ.

I hold that we ought to adopt the second view (that Jesus was unable to sin) for the following reasons. (a) If Jesus had been able to sin he must have had evil inclinations to which he might have succumbed. But if he had possessed these he would not have been sinless. He could then not have been the Redeemer; he himself would have needed redemption. (b) The idea that Jesus was constantly engaged in a moral struggle with a lower nature — with lust, envy, greed, sheer self-centredness and so on — is entirely incompatible with the Gospels' portrait of him. (c) If Jesus might have sinned he might have evaded the cross with all its shame and agony. And so God's purpose of redemption through him might have been frustrated. But can we think of this purpose in this way? Let us take, for example, our country's victory over Nazism. If some events that did occur had not occurred, or other events that did not occur had occurred, the victory might not have been achieved. Jesus, by analogy, might not have emerged victorious over evil; and the Gospel might never have come to be. (d) If Jesus was God incarnate — if (in patristic terminology) in him a human nature was hypostatically united with the divine nature in the person of the divine Son — he could not have either committed actual sin or possessed those evil impulses, creating evil motives and intentions, that the moral will opposes. To put it in other words, if Christ's human life was also fully and inseparably the life of God, it must have reflected, in modes appropriate to its historical particularity, divine goodness and self-giving.

I shall now examine some possible objections to the view I have stated.

It may be said that if Christ was not able to sin he did not possess free will and so in this respect was lacking in humanity. I do not find this objection convincing. The capacity to sin does not belong to human nature as such; it belongs only to human nature in the latter's present state. After death there will be no free choices between good and evil, no continuation of our present struggle with evil. Here we must distinguish between two senses of freedom. There is the free will whereby we are able to choose between good and evil. There is also freedom from all evil desires so that we spontaneously desire and do the good. Freedom in the first sense is given to us by God as a condition of our moral growth; but it is only a means towards obtaining freedom in the second sense whereby our minds and wills are permeated by love for God and of other human beings in him. Jesus, in possessing the second form of freedom but not the first, anticipates the heavenly life that awaits his disciples.

There is a further, general, point of Christology that needs to be made here. Although the human nature of Christ was structurally identical with ours in being characterized by both mind and body and, moreover, by an individual mind and an individual body, it also differed from ours in other ways. The principal and determinative difference was constituted by the sheer fact of the hypostatic union. Christ's humanity existed through, and only through, the Word's assumption of it from Christ's first moment of conception; it had no being independent of this union. One effect of this union was that the human Jesus was entirely sinless. A further effect was that he was able to redeem others while he himself had no need of redemption.

The second objection is perhaps the stronger one. It is also, I think, the one that is more likely to be urged. This is that if Jesus was necessarily sinless he could not have been tempted. The author of the epistle to the Hebrews writes thus, according to the Revised Standard Version:

> For we have not a high priest who is unable to sympathize with our weaknesses, but one who in every respect has been tempted as we are, yet without sinning. Let us then with confidence draw near to the throne of grace, that we may receive mercy and find grace to help in time of need.   (4: 15–16)

In order to clarify the matter we must make a verbal distinction. The Greek verb here can be translated either 'tempt' or 'test', and in this passage the New English Bible translates 'test'. The cognate noun correspondingly can be translated either 'test' (or 'trial') or 'temptation'. In common usage these are not necessarily the same. An examination is a test, perhaps indeed a trial. But it is not a temptation. So, far from appealing to what is morally bad in a candidate it is meant to elicit what is intellectually good.

We can certainly say that Christ's obedience and faith were tested and tried. They were so by many factors acting singly or together — by weariness, misunderstanding, loneliness, rejection and at the last the pain of the cross. In all these ways Christ himself was an example for Christians of whom the author of I Peter wrote:

> In this you rejoice, though now for a little while you may have to suffer various trials, so that the genuineness of your faith, more precious than gold which though perishable is tested by fire, may redound to praise and glory and honour at the revelation of Jesus Christ.   (1: 6–7)

Yet can we say that Jesus was tempted to do evil and to put his own will before the will of God? I maintain we cannot do so. If there was ever a case when Jesus could have been tempted to 'give up', to compromise, to evade the worst, it was at Gethsemane. Yet even there, having prayed in great distress of soul, 'Abba, Father, all things are possible to thee; remove this cup from me', he immediately added 'yet not what I will, but what thou wilt' (Mark 14: 36). Yet to affirm that Christ was not tempted is not to affirm that he was not tried. Also the former affirmation need not at all lead us to underestimate either the mental and physical strength of Christ's final testing or the cost to him of his victory over it.

What, then, are we to say of the so-called 'temptations' that, according to Matthew and Luke, Jesus experienced at the beginning of his ministry? Here we must move carefully. Whether, or how far, the references to Satan are to be taken literally or symbolically is a question that I shall leave open. I am concerned only to make basic points that remain. We must note first that these narratives are brief. They do not describe

Christ's 'inner state' throughout the forty days. We must note
too that these are specifically 'messianic' 'temptations' that can
be called 'messianic' 'tests' or 'trials' both because (as the
references to Deuteronomy show) they recall the testing of
Israel in the wilderness and because they 'tested' Christ's understanding of his vocation as the messiah and the one in whom
God's purpose for Israel was fulfilled. The question that faced
Jesus was this. How was he to discharge this vocation? By
performing a spectacular sign, by miraculously feeding the
hungry, by a display of military force? According to the evangelists, Jesus immediately rejected all these means as being
contrary to his Father's will.[3] We have good reason (especially
in the light of Luke 4:1-3) for holding that Jesus continued to
be thus 'tested'. Such continued 'testing' gives meaning to the
statement in Hebrews 5:8 that although Jesus was the divine
Son of God 'he learned obedience through what he suffered'.
We must take this to mean, not that Jesus was ever disobedient
(as we are) or tempted to disobey (as we are), but that through
his experiences he came increasingly to realize that he was to
fulfil his obedience as the suffering servant of the Lord. Finally
in order to understand these messianic trials we must realize
two further facts. First, the courses of action that Jesus rejected
were not intrinisically evil. On the contrary they could plausibly be represented as good. Thus the Jews were familiar from
their own writings with belief in a warrior messiah who would
destroy the Gentile oppressor and restore terrestrial glory to
Israel. Secondly, the Synoptic Gospels clearly indicate that
Jesus did not possess from the beginning a certain knowledge of
his destiny, but that even towards the end (until his final 'test'
at Gethsemane) he hoped that Israel would respond to the
message of the Kingdom that he had proclaimed and, beyond
proclaiming, enacted in his relation with all those whom he
encountered.

The so-called 'temptations' of Jesus, then, are better called
'tests'. C.H. Dodd, in his last book, states their meaning and
result as follows.

> At each stage we are reminded of incidents in which Israel was
> tested in the wilderness, and now the Israel-to-be, in the person
> of the messiah (the Servant of the Lord) is put to the test. But
> where ancient Israel failed to pass the test, he stands firm.[4]

Both because these were messianic tests and because Jesus
survived them, not merely without sinning, but also without
being tempted to sin, they differed from the temptations that
we experience. The diference can be expressed in terms of
Acton's dictum that 'power tends to corrupt and absolute
power corrupts absolutely'. Not even the most powerful tyrant
possesses absolute power in the strict sense of 'absolute'
(although we here naturally apply the adjective to such tyrants
as Stalin and Hitler). 'Absolute' power belongs only to the
divine Father and his incarnate Son. The point then is this.
Although power tends to corrupt us and in its extreme forms
can corrupt completely, it did not corrupt the only man to
whom strictly absolute power was given. He did not merely not
misuse power for his own ends or the ends of his nation Israel.
He did not misuse it even for his Father's ends when it was clear
to him that he must accomplish his Father's saving will solely
through sacrificial love.

There is, however, a major qualification that must be made
here. I left open the question whether Satan exists and so
whether Christ encountered him in the wilderness even if the
encounter did not occur exactly as it is described by the evangelists. If Satan exists and there was such an encounter we can
obviously say that from Satan's viewpoint Jesus was tempted.
By this I mean that it was Satan's aim to tempt Jesus by
proposing courses of action that, though they might seem to be
desirable, were in fact contrary to the will of God. In making
them seem desirable Satan characteristically disguised himself
as an angel of light. However, in thinking that he could tempt
Jesus, Satan was mistaken; and so he had lost the battle before
it had begun. Of course if Satan exists and tempts us he does so
really and sometimes with 'demonic' effects by appealing to
those sinful impulses in us that impede our communion with
God and prompt us to disobey his will.

It may, however, now be said that if Christ did not experience our temptations, if he was free from every evil desire
and the slightest tendency to prefer his own will to the will of
God, we cannot make sense of the statements in Hebrews that
'because he himself has suffered and been tempted, he is able to
help those who are tempted' and that 'we have not an high
priest who is unable to sympathize with our weaknesses, but

one who in every respect has been tempted as we are, yet without sinning' (Hebrews 2:18 and 4:15, RSV). However, the New English Bible (as I have observed with reference to the second statement) here translates 'test'. Its full translations are 'for since he himself has passed through the test of suffering, he is able to help those who are meeting their test now' and 'for ours is not a high priest unable to sympathize with our weaknesses, but one who, because of his likeness to us, has been tested every way, only without sin'. The exalted Christ, then, sympathizes with us in our trials because of those that he endured at the cost of the mental and physical sufferings that the evangelists record.

Yet Christ's sympathy would not itself be enough to make him the Redeemer. The author of Hebrews continued thus in 4:16, 'Let us then with confidence draw near to the throne of grace, that we may receive mercy and find grace to help in time of need'. If we interpret these words Christologically and with reference to Christ's sinlessness their meaning is as follows. We, unlike Christ, are tempted by sinful impulses; and we, unlike Christ therefore, often surrender to them. We therefore need his divine forgiveness and aid. In offering us his sympathy Christ is related to us as his brethren. In needing his grace we are related to him as our Lord.

The account of Christ's sinlessness I have offered is of general significance for Christology. Our understanding of him must be based on a recognition that he was both like and unlike us. He was like us in so far as he possessed an individual mind and body, thought in concepts taken from his cultural background, was forced to come to terms with his historical circumstances, knew God by faith and not sight, and was tested by evil. He was unlike us in so far as his whole life was governed by the Godhead to which it was indissolubly united; so that all his acts were simultaneously acts of God. As the incarnation of the Son he was a finite emobodiment of the infinite love that he enjoys with the Father (to whom he therefore offered himself completely) and with the Holy Spirit (by whom therefore he was completely possessed). An excessive stress on the unlikeness can lead, implicitly if not explicitly, to a Monophysite and Docetic view of him whereby his humanity is suppressed by his deity and is more apparent than real. An excessive stress on his likeness can lead to a merely human view of him as one who can help us in our war against sin only to the extent that he is an inspiring example.

In concluding, I shall attempt to deal with a further question thay may be raised. Was Jesus the only person who has lived and ever will live a wholly sinless life? The full doctrine of original sin affirms that on account of Adam's 'fall' all men are sinners, in the sense of being in the grip of sinful impulses. It is, however, doubtful whether even if there was such a 'fall', belief in it entails the view that all Adam's descendants are thereby vitiated. Moreover, if we do not believe in such a fall we do not have (so far as I can see) any a priori ground for affirming that all men are sinful. Yet there is a vast amount of empirical evidence for maintaining that sinfulness is universal in the sense that it is so widely and so insidiously present in every type of man and every type of society that a wholly sinless person would be (to say the least) a startling exception.[5] Certainly the experience of Christians from the beginning has been both that they have sinful impulses and that they freely commit actual sins by yielding to the latter. The author of 1 John sums it up thus:

> If we say we have no sin, we deceive ourselves and the truth is not in us. If we confess our sins, he is faithful and just, and will forgive our sins and cleanse us from all unrighteousness.
>
> (1. 8–9)[6]

In my view the question whether there have been, or are, or will be sinless persons apart from Christ is one that no human mind can answer. In any case his sinlessness was unique *per se* through his hypostatic union with the divine Son, in its necessity (constituted by this union), and in its redemptive effects.

1 English trans. Edinburgh, T & T Clark, 1968. Thus on p.361 Schleiermacher writes that redemption is effected by Jesus 'through the communication of his sinless perfection'. I quote Schleiermacher because in so many ways he can be regarded as the origin of modern theology.

2 The memory of Christ's divinely inspired goodness is reflected in the primitive kerygma. Thus Peter is recorded as proclaiming 'how God anointed Jesus of Nazareth with the Holy Spirit and with power; how he

went about doing good and healing all that were oppressed by the devil, for God was with him' (Acts 10:38).

3 Jesus later refused to grant the Pharisees a 'sign from heaven' (Mark 8: 11–12). Admittedly he miraculously fed the five thousand. But for him this was a spontaneous act of compassion that, like his other miracles, must be placed in the total context of his teaching and self-understanding. Moreover, according to the fourth evangelist, when the people who had witnessed the miracle wanted to make him king he immediately sought solitude and told them to desire, not material, but spiritual bread made available to him as 'the bread of life' (John 6:15ff).

4 *The Founder of Christianity* (London, Collins, 1971, pp. 107–8).

5 According to the dogma of the Immaculate Conception, Mary was such an exception; she was from the first moment of her conception kept free from every stain of original sin. But most of the great schoolmen (including Aquinas) rejected the belief.

6 Belief in original sin has been defended on grounds that do not imply belief in Adam's 'fall'. Thus Augustine appealed to biblical texts additional to Genesis, to the tradition of the Church, and to the wickedness he found in the world around him. For a recent restatement of the belief from a philosophical point of view see Iris Murdoch's *The Sovereignty of Good* (London, Routledge & Kegan Paul, 1970, pp.50–51)

William James and the Notion of Two Worlds

D.Z. PHILLIPS

Life, like a dome of many-coloured glass,
Stains the white radiance of eternity.

Shelley, *Adonais*

How do philosophers discuss Shelley's figure of a higher and lower reality? Some have said that the higher reality is beyond the reach of human beings. It is said that there is something about the very conditions under which we live our lives which makes it impossible for this higher reality to be grasped. If this thesis is put baldly, with such a sharp distinction between higher and lower that the higher reality is said to be incomprehensible, an immediate difficulty occurs. How do we ever come to a conception of this higher reality in the first place? To avoid this difficulty it is thought that, somehow or other, what is higher must be thought to break in on what is lower. If such a breakthrough is assumed, however, can the higher reality still be thought of as an inscrutable mystery? This difficulty, in its turn, is thought to be avoided by saying that the higher reality undergoes certain modifications as it breaks through. The figure of the dome is that of human life as necessarily distorting. Yet, taken in one way, the figure only postpones the difficulty, for if the higher reality is said to be distorted, how is the distortion to be recognized? In order to recognize something as a distortion, we seem to need an independent acquaintance with that which is said to be distorted.

These are the traditional difficulties which arise if we think of the distinction between a higher and a lower reality as a distinction between two realms, even between two places, a 'here' and a 'somewhere else'. The difficulties seem to be difficulties of communication: how does the higher reality become known in the lower realm? We shall see, however, that this assumption is deeply misleading. The difficulty facing us is not one of communication, but of conception. This may not be apparent immediately, since conceptual difficulties often take the outward form of difficulties of communication. What needs to be examined is the initial assumption that we are confronted by two distinct categories, a higher and a lower reality, and that our task is to try to establish some kind of relation between these categories.

These issues can be clarified by considering the way in which William James understood Shelley's poetic figure. He wants to submit Shelley's words to an empiricist query. He asks, 'But is it really so?' James makes the fundamental assumption that Shelley's words are a description, the truth of which is to be checked over against some kind of reality. To ask whether Shelley's description is really so, is to ask whether the check is affirmative. The affirmative check depends on the prior truth of some state of affairs. Since the state of affairs in question, however, is said to be beyond our world, no direct check is possible. The best we have is a form of speculation or sup-position. James makes a frank admission that this is so. James says of Shelley's words:

> Suppose, now, that this were really so, and suppose, moreover, that the dome, opaque enough at all times to the full super-solar blaze, could at certain times and places grow less so, and let certain beams pierce through into this sublunary world. These beams would be so many finite rays, so to speak, of consciousness, and they would vary in quantity and quality as the opacity varied in degree. Only at particular times and places would it seem that, as a matter of fact, the veil of nature can grow thin and rupturable enough for such effects to occur. But in these places gleams, however finite and unsatisfying, of the absolute life of the universe, are from time to time vouchsafed. Glows of feeling, glimpses of insight, and streams of knowledge and perception that float into our finite world.

> (On Psychical Research)[1]

This, then, is how James understands Shelley's words. Something like this must be true, he thinks, if there is to be any truth in his words. The next step, for James, is to check whether the communications give evidence for the existence of a higher reality. But where does the conception of the higher reality come from? Is it a supposition or conviction? Perhaps it could even be called faith. The faith cannot emanate from the evidence, since the evidence is supposed to give that faith something it lacks, namely, a proof or a foundation. On this view, then, faith is faith in a hypothesis. For example, faith in the reality of the dead, on this view, is faith in a hypothesis. What is needed is proof, and it is the possibility of such proof that James investigates. He thinks that such proof should be scientific, and that the science which is to provide it is psychical research.

At first, it looks as if James is embarking on a kind of enterprise with which we are familiar, but an enterprise on a vaster scale. It is not the investigation of another planet, however distant, and yet it is supposed to be the investigation of another region, a 'somewhere else'. Yet, when we try to look at James's enquiry in this way, various anomalies confront us. On the one hand, James insists that his enquiry is scientific and he criticizes other scientists for their narrowness in not heeding it. On the other hand, we find him admitting that, at a theoretical level, he made little progress. What James means by 'little progress', however, is not what a scientist may mean when he says that he is making little progress in testing a hypothesis within an established scientific procedure. Neither is it similar to what might be meant by saying that little progress had been made in seeking a radical shift or extension in some branch of science. What James is saying is that he had made little progress in seeing how his enquiries can be called scientific at all. It is unclear to what extent James recognizes the nature of his difficulties. His is not a lack of progress within procedures endowed with scientific sense, but a lack of progress in endowing his procedures with a scientific sense in the first place. His problem is not lack of progress within the sense of his procedures, but lack of progress with the issue of what sense, if any, his procedures have. I need to give evidence for this view of James's difficulties. I also want to show that had James given a certain kind of attention to the phenomena which lay before him, he, too, could have come to see his difficulties in this light.

As I have said, James was critical of the attitude of many

scientists, physiologists, psychologists and medical men in turning their backs on psychical phenomena. James wanted to insist on there being a reality beyond anything the sciences were prepared to recognize.

> The ideal of every science is a closed and completed system of truth...Each one of our various *ologies* seems to offer a definite head of classification for every possible phenomenon of the sort which it professes to cover; and so far from free is most men's fancy, that, when a consistent and organised scheme of this sort has once been comprehended and assimilated, a different scheme is unimaginable. No alternative, whether to whole or parts, can any longer be conceived as possible. Phenomena unclassifiable within the system are therefore paradoxical absurdities, and must be held untrue.   (p.26)

On the other hand, James did not think the phenomena with which he was concerned involved realities different in kind from those which occupy scientists. Otherwise, his appeal to scientists would have little point. James was not denying the possibility of a science of the mystical. On the contrary, he was appealing for one. He wanted the sciences to which he appealed to extend their procedures to include psychical phenomena. In fact he claimed that the 'Society for Psychical Research has been one means of bringing science and the occult together' (p.28).

The vital question, for James, is precisely how an extension from the sciences to the occult is to be brought about: 'What science needs is a *context* to make the trance phenomena continuous with other physiological and psychological facts' (p.98). But James never found this context. He had to admit defeat. The best evidence which he thought came his way was the experiences of a medium called Mrs Piper with whom he was particularly impressed. But even of her evidence he said 'In the trances of this medium, I cannot resist the conviction that knowledge appears which she has never gained by the ordinary waking use of her eyes and ears and wits. What the source of this knowledge may be I know not, and have not the glimmer of an explanatory suggestion to make' (p.98). The situation with respect to a search for explanation did not change. To provide a theoretical context for the phenomena which interested him remained an insurmountable obstacle for James. He is as honest as ever in his admission of this fact:

> For twenty-five years I have been in touch with the literature of
> psychical research, and have had acquaintance with numerous
> 'researchers'. I have also spent a good many hours (though far
> fewer than I ought to have spent) in witnessing (or trying to
> witness) phenomena. Yet I am theoretically no 'further' than I
> was at the beginning, and I confess that at times I have been
> tempted to believe that the Creator has eternally intended this
> department of nature to remain *baffling*, to prompt our curiosities
> and hopes and suspicions all in equal measure, so that, although
> ghosts and clairvoyances, and raps and messages from spirits, are
> always seeming to exist and can never be fully explained away,
> they also can never be susceptible of full corroboration. (p.310)

What, then, did James do faced with these theoretical dead
ends? With modesty, he said, 'I can only arrange the material'
(p.148). No doubt, in contrast to the hope for a full explanatory
theory, arranging the material seemed to be straightforward
enough. Yet, it is the seemingly straightforward which often
misleads and confuses us. Despite his claim, the last thing James
does is simply to arrange the material which confronts him. He
does not wait on the material; he does not let it speak for itself.
For example, James never thought of asking whether the failure
to fit the phenomena in question into a theoretical framework,
might be due to a misunderstanding and misrepresentation of
these phenomena. He never questioned that the phenomena
should be treated in impersonal, theoretical terms. For James,
deciding whether a message is from the dead is similar logically,
despite all the difficulties, to tracing the source of other
messages. Of course, it is not as simple as tracing the source of
a telephone message, but, nevertheless, tracing the source is the
task which it is thought confronts us.

Why did James not look elsewhere for other possibilities of
characterizing the material which confronted him? Some possibilities, perhaps, were ruled out from the outset because of
James's relation to religion. He said of himself, 'You see,
although religion is the great interest of my life, I am rather
hopelessly non-evangelical and take the whole thing too imper-
sonally' (p.262). I suppose we could say that there is a hint in
this confession that James wondered at times whether his
characterization and treatment of the phenomena which interested him were wholly appropriate.

Yet, we need not rely on such hints in questioning James's treatment of psychical phenomena. There are features of the phenomena themselves, features which James himself noticed, which should have led him to question his methods. In discussing the issue of the reality of a spirit-world, James tells us why he is worried about treating psychic phenomena as evidence. The trouble, James said, is that '"spirits" of any grade, although they are indeed matters of tradition, seem to have shown themselves (as far as concrete evidence for them goes) nowhere except in the specific phenomena under investigation' (p.145). For James, the psychic phenomena are hints, bits of evidence, of the reality of spirits. What does not seem possible is to check the appearances against the reality. Clearly, it would be a great help if, now and again, spirits could be encountered directly, as it were, independent of any medium or psychic phenomena. We could then check the veracity or otherwise of appearances against our acquaintance with the reality in question. But all we have are appearances. James regrets the fact that we have mediated, but no direct, experience of spirits. James believes it to be a contingent fact that the showing forth of spirits is confined to psychic phenomena. The spirits could show themselves directly, but, for reasons we do not comprehend, they happen not to, that is all.

Here we have an excellent example of how mystery can be brought in in the wrong place. James wants to confront the source of the mysteries directly, as it were. He wants to perceive spirits. The mediation of spirits is seen as an unfortunate hindrance. What James would like to eliminate, however, may turn out to be one context which grounds conditions of intelligibility where talk of spirits is concerned. He never considers the possibility that what is meant by a showing forth of the spirits is internally related to those contexts in which people speak of psychic phenomena. The reason why spirits do not appear directly, outside such contexts, may not be, as James thought, a contingent fact. It may well be that it makes no sense to speak of spirits appearing outside these contexts, since it is in these contexts that the notion of the appearance of spirits has its sense. What James took to be a contingent fact about the behaviour of spirits may turn out to be an indication of the conceptual parameters within which talk of spirits has sense.

While James recognized that spirits are a matter of tradition, as he put it, he paid too little attention to the kind of discourse the tradition exemplified.

What happens if we do pay attention to the contexts in which talk of 'spirits showing forth' has sense? Certainly, we shall find that they are very mixed in character. At one end of the spectrum are those which James would be all too ready to acknowledge as involving frauds and deceivers. At the other end of the spectrum, however, we find examples with features which James half-recognized; features, which, if he had given them full insight, would have involved James in a radical change of direction. James realized that even if his enquiries into psychical phenomena were as successful as he could have hoped, he would still have probabilities, conjectures, no more. He also saw that man's faith in another world did not take the form of faith in probabilities and conjectures. Looking at his own methods of enquiry, James said '...only possibilities are opened, and what most men want are certainties' (p.267). Of course, for James, this was a matter of precipitate judgement on the part of most men. He never considered that the kind of certainty men seek may be related to the kind of reality believed in, as in, for example, absolute belief in the reality of the dead. Such a belief can be found in Shelley's poem, the poem which James turns into a theory:

> I am borne darkly, fearfully, afar;
> Whilst, burning through the inmost veil of Heaven,
> The soul of Adonais, like a star
> Beacons from the abode where the Eternal are.

But James need not have turned to Shelley. Indeed, he need not have turned to anyone else at all. Features on which he needed to concentrate can be found in his own attitude. According to Gardner Murphy, James, at the end, while retaining his empiricist assumptions, despaired at the lack of theoretical advance in his enquiries. He turned elsewhere to distinguish between the authentic and the sham in psychic phenomena. As I have said, James was ruthless in wanting to expose deceivers and poseurs. On the other hand, he came to think that whatever is meant by an authoritative appearance of spirits, it was a misunderstanding to seek support for such appearances which would be quite independent of the context in which it is said to occur. In what direction, then, did his thought turn? According to Gardner Murphy,

> James feels his way to the position that it is not essentially the mass of evidential material, but something about the exquisite rendering of the personal quality of... individuality, as it deals gently with certain... memories, that constitutes the best evidence of its survival. James was groping toward the view expressed by many since his time, that there is something about the style of personality modulation that properly carries its own conviction, as in recognising a voice over the telephone or in recognising the style of a master in the arts when sheer analysis of content or structure must fail. (p.330)

In these remarks, there are still misplaced analogies. It is still important that, independently of the quality of the voice on the telephone, the call can still be traced; independently of one's impressions of a master's art, the history of the work can be traced. The detection of hoaxes and forgeries depends, often, on such independent checks. James, on the other hand, was moving more and more towards relying on the qualitative characteristics of the whole situation in which psychic phenomena occur, in determining the authority and authenticity of the phenomena in question. Murphy regretted this change of direction in James, a change which, to him, was a departure from scientific propriety. He says, 'In view of the unknown riches of histrionic skill which a medium like Mrs Piper may have been able to command, this argument does not carry today the insight which James attached to it fifty years ago' (p.330). These remarks were made in 1958, but nothing since has made Murphy's reaction any less common. Earlier in his life, James had made similar criticisms of Frederic Myers. Myers, James had said, 'so habitually saw the meanest subliminal phenomena in the light of that transterrane world with which they might remotely be connected, that they became glorified in his mind into experiences in themselves majestic. All his materials were objects of love to him...' (p.236). Myers' emotional involvement in his subject, was, for James, a matter to be regretted. At this stage, James neither had this involvement, nor considered it relevant. James did not ask whether the emotional involvement, so far from being a distorting intrusion, is the kind of precondition necessary in order for the phenomena in question to be part of one's experience. Perhaps proof here, as Kierkegaard said of religion, is from the emotions. If this were the case, to say that Myers' materials were objects of love to him would be simply to note the aspect under which his materials are to be understood. Such an aspect would not depend on tracing messages from the dead by analogy with tracing human messages, except in this case the tracing is of a remoter connection. Whether the connections the aspect in question allows one to make are called 'glorifications of the mind' depends on the surroundings of the case in question. No a priori judgement can be made. In some cases, the surroundings may lead one to speak of delusions or hallucinations. In other cases it would be unclear what such judgements would amount to.[2]

I am not claiming more for James than that, at the end, there seemed to be the beginnings of moves in a new direction. Had these moves developed, he would have given greater attention to what the medium actually said and to how the words are taken up into the lives of those who hear them. Certain questions may then be asked: What would lead us to call certain reactions experiencing hallucinations? What would lead someone to say that the message is from a dead one? These questions will lead to different answers in different circumstances. What is strange, however, given the accounts of messages from the dead given in psychical research, is that acceptance of the message as coming from a dead one does *not* depend on attempts to trace the source of the message. Notice, this is not because the notion of a source is unimportant. Clearly, it is. If, for example, someone believed that his own grief was the cause of the alleged message, it could not be accepted as a message from the dead. It is essential to the authority of the message that it is from the dead. What is at issue is the grammar or logic of 'from the dead'. What I am suggesting is that the grammar involved is such that any notion of 'tracing the message' distorts and misunderstands it.

Let us consider some examples. First, an example which involves the reality of the dead, but which does not involve, necessarily, any notion of the presence of the dead one or any notion of the spirit of the dead one speaking to one. I am

thinking of the way in which Kierkegaard speaks of the trans-
figured will of a dead one; the way in which moral obligations
to a person may transcend death. Either one comes to terms
with the moral will of the dead one or does not; there is no
bargaining with it. Someone, who finds this moral relation
puzzling, may ask why someone desists now from doing something which, during his father's lifetime he had argued for
doing. 'Why have you stopped doing it now?' he may be asked.
He replies, 'My father disapproves'. 'But' his questioner retorts,
'Your father is dead'. Comes the reply, 'Exactly!'

The example of the obligation to a dead person comes nearer
to those which we are discussing if we think of the person
thinking of himself living his life in the presence of the dead
father; under his watchful eye, he might say. When he does
wrong, he says that his dead father censures him. Here, again,
the notion of the presence of the father is one which cannot be
broken down further. Its sense is mediated through the moral
concerns which surround it. But if we begin to ask how exactly
the dead father could see the son's misdeeds, etc. we go down
a road which distorts the example I have outlined.

Again, consider the following example. Schumann was convinced that he was in touch with the spirit of Schubert. Here,
the claim has sense in the context of certain musical traditions
of composition. Here, one may be able to see how the notion of
a composition being inspired by the spirit of a dead composer
may have application. If we could call the music and the
composition the medium in this case, then it could be said that
the medium is not the means by which two realms are brought
into contact with each other, but, rather, the context in which
the idea of such a contact gets its sense. What would it mean to
say the contact is illusory? Would this be anything more than
a refusal to speak as Schumann did of his composition? If a man
claims to be hearing voices which claim to give him messages
in the ways in which the person standing next to him might give
him a message, we have familiar ways of checking out his claim.
But do we have the same procedures for deciding when a
composer is or is not in touch with the spirit of a dead composer.
One can imagine the claim being denied if his music is bad!

Think again of an example of sharing experiences with the
dead. I heard of a devoted married couple who travelled exten-

sively, their main interest being church architecture. They had a photograph of a church which interested them, but they did not know its location. They hoped to find the church one day, but when the husband died they still had not done so. His wife, along with another widow, continued her travels. One day she discovered the church in the photograph. She turned to her side, where no one was standing, and said, 'Here's our church'.[3] Whenever she found the church, it would be a shared finding. But, once again, if we start asking about the exact location of her husband at her side, we would be distorting the situation.

No doubt it will be said that examples of the kind we are considering are free from features such as apparitions, strange voices, familiar voices coming through the medium, etc., etc. After looking at these phenomena, it is said, an explanation must be sought. How could the medium know facts known only to the client and the dead person? How does the voice of the dead person come from the medium's mouth? How do the appearances come about? If certain explanations are given in reply to these questions, the phenomena cease to be regarded as authentic psychic phenomena. If we find out that someone has told the medium of the so-called secret after all; if we find that the medium is imitating the voice of the dead person; if we find that the appearances or sounds have been staged; then the authenticity of the phenomena will be rejected. The inexplicable character of the phenomena is a necessary feature of them. The difficulty is that people speak as if there were an explanation, but one yet to be worked out. After the description of the phenomena, some people then say, 'Therefore...' and proceed to give a theory in terms of psychic communication. The difficulty, as William James recognized, is in the assumption surrounding the 'therefore'. It may seem as if the 'therefore' establishes a connection between the phenomena and a form of explanation logically akin to forms of explanation with which we are familiar. But as James had to admit after twenty years of enquiry, the nature of such an explanatory extension is logically problematic. What we are left with, then, are the inexplicable phenomena, but without a 'therefore' leading to any form of explanation. What we make of the phenomena then depends on the role they play in people's lives. Even in the absence of explanation some people ask, 'But what *is* happening?' almost as if concentrating on the inexplicable phenomenon itself is what sustains them. But, then, this simply postpones the question of the style in which they are sustained, a style which can range from idle curiosity to reverence.

People's readings of the phenomena in question will vary. A man may claim that he is visited by his dead father, while others may say that his claim is the product of emotional dependence. When he is in trouble, he blames the spirit of his dead father which, he says, possesses him. Those who criticize him deny that he is in contact with his father. But what is the ground for their judgement? The lack of independent evidence? But, as James points out, other examples may lack such evidence too. The idea of the lack of such evidence comes into its own in the identification of hallucinations and delusions. The problem comes in the extension of these categories to cases where other factors are involved. Are the voices which Joan of Arc said she heard hallucinations? How is that question to be answered?[4] In the case we are considering, the qualitative character of the relationship with the dead father seems to be the determining factor in concluding that the person is not in contact with his dead father, but is in the grip of emotional dependence. Others might read the situation differently. Why should relationships with the dead or the presence of the spirits of the dead be confined to the kind of ethical example Kierkegaard discusses? Why not say in the other cases, too, that the surroundings show what the reality of the dead comes to in this context? After all, the spirits of the dead need not be benign. We are reminded of the oppressive presence of the dead parents to whom R.S. Thomas introduces us in the terrible family he depicts:

> John All and his lean wife,
> Whose forced complicity gave life
> To each loathed foetus, stare from the wall,
> Dead not absent. The night falls.[5]

The same considerations apply to the various games people play concerning the dead. But how does the game enter their lives? If they say, 'It's only a game' this would be a reason for saying that the notion of the reality of the dead does not enter their lives. If, however, the game does enter their lives in various ways, then the role it plays may affect what people say about their contact with the dead. These roles may be ethical, emotional, profound, shallow, evil, curious, shabby, trivial, etc., etc.

What I hope to show in these various examples is that the relation between what might be meant by visitations from the dead and people's active responses is not an external one. It would therefore be a misunderstanding to think that we could first establish the reality or otherwise of the spirits of the dead and then, in the light of our findings, determine the appropriateness of the various responses. The reason why this is so should be obvious by now, namely, that, often, it is only in the context of such responses that the particular talk of the reality of the dead has its home. These contexts are not descriptions of a further reality external to themselves. On the contrary, they constitute the grammatical parameters which determine what the distinction between 'real' and 'unreal' amounts to here.

No doubt some will conclude, as a result of the way I have argued, that an individual may choose to mean whatever he likes by the reality of the dead, and that no room remains for the determination of truth and falsity. These conclusions do not follow. Apart from the example where those involved regard the whole thing as a harmless game, in none of the examples we have considered would the people involved say that the question of the reality of the dead is determined by their say-so. The beliefs could not be taken up or discarded at will. There is room within the examples for the distinction between truth and falsity. Judgements could be made in these contexts between allegiance and deniance, integrity and self-deception, genuineness and distortion. Whether these beliefs can become truths for an individual depends on whether he can feed on them.

What would James's reactions have been to the examples I have considered? Despite the hints in his last thoughts to which I have referred, I suspect that he would have said of them what he said of Myers' way of talking, namely, that they are products of the imagination, a 'glorification of the mind'. Recall what James did to Shelley's poetic imagination. He turned it into a theory. He failed to take seriously the primacy of the poetic figure. He made the figure an hypothesis awaiting further confirmation. What would not have been a product of imagination for James would have been some kind of scientific confirmation of psychic phenomena. I have attempted to show why such a distinction between what does and does not belong to the imagination in this context is problematic.

But what of James's empiricist question, 'But is it really so?' Is there no room for such a question, not simply *within*, but as *between* the various contexts I have outlined? If, as I have argued, it is a misunderstanding to think of the parameters of meaning we have considered as descriptions of a further reality, what can the question 'But is it really so?' mean? We will not be able to answer the question as if we have a hypothesis which could be settled by an agreed common method of assessment. The question 'But is it really so?', however, may be a question about the sense of what is going on. It may be that investigation will reveal conceptual confusions of a kind which will lead one to say, not that the belief in the reality of the dead is false (which assumes that one could make sense of its truth), but that the belief is meaningless. I have argued that it is impossible to say that all the examples I have considered are the products of conceptual confusion. Even if all such confusions were cleared up, there would still be an irreducible variety of beliefs beyond such criticism.

For similar reasons one could not say that all the examples we have considered are products of the imagination in a pejorative sense. The readiness to do so would at least have to take into account the fact that *within* the examples considered we already have a distinction between what is and what is not a product of imagination. Consider the belief that one's dead father watches over one. Clearly, substituting, 'I imagined that my dead father was watching over me' will not do, since that amounts to a denial. Neither could one say that the belief is the product of one's imaginative insight, since the emphasis then seems to be on oneself and not on the will of the dead father. Again, the phrase, 'It is as if my dead father watches over me' will not do, since it does not have the same bearing on one's life as 'My dead father watches over me'. Why should it be thought that a substitute expression can be found here? If distinctions between what does and does not belong to the imagination operate within the parameters of use of these expressions, what would it mean to call the parameters themselves a product of imagination?

The question 'But is it really so?' has other applications. First, it can be asked by those who reject on moral, religious or aesthetic grounds, these different beliefs in the reality of the dead. They find the beliefs shabby, superficial. Struck by the banality and triviality of so many messages said to be from the dead, they shrug and pass on. To ask 'But is it really so?' is to ask whether one can accord the required status to the belief in question. The kind of reaction I have in mind is well illustrated by some remarks by T.H. Huxley which James quotes, but does not appreciate. Huxley says,

> ... even supposing these phenomena to be genuine — they do not interest me... The only good that I can see in the demonstration of the 'Truth of Spiritualism' is to furnish an additional argument against suicide. Better live a crossing-sweeper, than die and be made to talk twaddle by a 'medium' hired at a guinea a *seance*. (p.315).

Huxley's reaction does not depend on falsifying any claims. It is a reaction which says, 'So what?' in face of the triviality it takes itself to be confronted by. Nothing said in this lecture rules out the possibility of such a judgement in face of what goes on in the majority of seances.

The question 'But is it really so?' may have an important place *within* various beliefs in the reality of the dead. It amounts to asking, 'Am I being fooled?' or 'Am I fooling myself?' Of course, these questions can be asked of trivial games, but I am thinking now of the way they may occur when I believe serious demands are made of me by the dead. Here, I wonder from time to time whether this does amount to anything. This kind of doubt is not uncommon where serious issues are at stake in one's life. The demand made on me may involve my giving up a great deal. I ask, 'But is it really so?' I am trying to get clear about what is being asked of me; trying to get certain issues into perspective. On the other hand, the struggle, simply in being what it is, reveals something of my own character and the character of my beliefs.

It should be clear from this essay why philosophy cannot tell people directly what they should make of beliefs in the reality of the dead. People differ in their reactions; agreement in reactions cannot be taken for granted. In bringing out the kinds of issues involved, the kinds of questions and judgements which are made, philosophy is clearing the ground in such a way as to allow these issues, judgements and questions to be themselves. In doing so, philosophy is not itself indulging in a game of assessing probabilities where beliefs in the reality of the dead are concerned.

William James, at the end of his enquiries, gave some small indication of a move in the direction which this essay has taken. He began to appreciate that if we are going to talk of mysteries, the sense of the mysteries must be mediated in the detail of human life. So little came of the indications James provides that it is difficult to know how much weight to give them. Whatever of this, the burden of my argument has been that it is in the direction, barely hinted at in James, that further clarity about the issues I have raised should be sought.[6]

1 William James, *On Psychical Research*, compiled and edited by Gardner Murphy and Robert O. Ballou, Chatto and Windus, 1961, pp.291–292. Subsequent page references throughout the chapter are to this work.

2 For the distinction between attitudes to the dead which can and cannot be regarded as projections of the mind see my *Religion Without Explanation*, Basil Blackwell, 1976, Chapter 8: 'Perspectives on the Dead'.

3 I was given this example or one very like it in a graduate seminar in the Department of Religious Studies at Carleton University, Ottawa in 1976.

4 For an excellent discussion of such questions see 'Religion and Madness' in M. O'C. Drury, *The Danger of Words*, Routledge and Kegan Paul, 1973, pp.116–137.

5 'Meet the Family' in R.S. Thomas, *Selected Poems 1946–1968*, Granada, 1979, p.55.

6 An earlier version of this paper was delivered as the 1982 William James Lecture at Louisiana State University.

A Bibliography of the Writings of Hywel D. Lewis*

1936

'Was Green a Hedonist? Discussion'. *Mind*, Vol. XLV, April, 1936. pp. 193–8.

'Lle'r Syniad o Werth Mewn Moeseg'. (The Concept of Value in Morality), *Y Llenor*, Cyf. XV, Gwanwyn (Spring) 1936, tt. 30–43.

'Y Bardd a'r Athronydd' (The Poet and the Philosopher), *Y Llenor*, Cyf. XV, Hydref (Autumn) 1936, tt. 145–55.

1937

'Some Observations on Natural Rights and the General Will — (1)', *Mind*, Vol. XLVI, October 1937, pp. 437–53.

'Y Gelfyddyd o Wrando', (The Art of Listening), *Traethodydd*, Cyf. VI, Gorffennaf (July) 1937, tt. 148–57.

'Meddylwyr Mawr y Byd — Aristoteles — (I)', (Great Thinkers of the World), *Efrydydd*, Cyf. III, Rhan I, 1937, tt. 42–54.

'Meddylwyr Mawr y Byd — Aristoteles — (2)', (Great Thinkers of the World), *Efrydydd*, Cyf. III, Rhan 2, 1937, tt. 35–43.

Review of Philip Leon, *The Ethics of Power* in *The International Journal of Ethics*, Vol. 47, July 1937, pp. 480–86.

1938

'Some Observations on Natural Rights and the General Will — (2)', *Mind*, Vol. XLVII, January 1938, pp. 18–44.

'Naive Realism and a Passage in the *Theaetetus*'. Discussion. *Mind*, Vol. XLVII, July 1938, pp. 351–6.

'Seiliau Athronyddol Rhyddid', (The Philosophical Basis of Freedom) *Tir Newydd*, Tachwedd (November) 1938, tt. 32–7.

Review of W.E. Hocking, *The Lasting Elements of Individualism* in *Hibbert Journal*, Vol. XXXVI, 1938, pp. 634–7.

*The editors express their grateful thanks to Alun Eurig Davies, Senior Sub-Librarian, The Library, University College of Wales, Aberystwyth for his assistance in compiling this bibliography.

Adolygiad (Review) o J.W. Gough, *The Social Contract* yn *Efrydiau Athronyddol*, Cyf. 1, 1938, tt. 85–7.

1939

'Plato and the Social Contract', *Mind*, Vol. XLVIII, January 1939, pp. 78–81.

'Beirniadaeth Adrodd — (I)' (Criticism of Recitation), *Y Llenor*, Cyf. 18, Haf (Summer) 1939, tt. 118–21.

'Beirniadaeth Adrodd — (2)' (Criticism of Recitation), *Y Llenor*, Cyf. 18, Hydref (Autumn) 1939, tt. 172–83.

'Syniadau Sylfaenol Athroniaeth Boliticaidd' (The Fundamental Ideas of Political Philosophy), *Efrydiau Athronyddol*, Cyf. 2, 1939, tt. 61–9.

1940

'Is There a Social Contract? — (I)', *Philosophy*, Vol. XV, 1940, pp. 64–79.

'The Original Contract', *Ethics*, Vol. L, January 1940, pp. 193–205.

'Culture and National Life', *Life and Letters Today*, 1940, pp. 236–44.

'Is There a Social Contract? — (2)', *Philosophy*, Vol. XV, April 1940, pp. 177–89.

Gweriniaeth (Republic), Llyfrau'r Methodistiaid Calfinaidd, 1940.

'Datblygiad Gwladwriaethau Cynnar' (The Development of States), *Traethodydd*, Cyf. XCV, Ionawr (January) 1940, tt. 49–57.

'Y Wladwriaeth yn Aeddfedu' (The Mature State), *Traethodydd*, Cyf. XCV, Rhif 415, Ebrill (April), 1940, tt. 81–93.

'Gwrthwynebu'r Wladwriaeth' (Resisting the State), *Efrydydd*, Cyf. 5, Rhif 3, Mawrth (March), 1940, tt. 21–7.

'Cyfrifoldeb Moesol a Rhyddid' (Moral Responsibility and Freedom), *Efrydiau Athronyddol*, Cyf. 3, 1940, tt. 3–20.

'Diwinyddion Heddiw – (I) Reinhold Niebuhr', (Theologians of Today, Reinhold Niebuhr), *Efrydydd*, Cyf. VI, Hydref (Autumn), 1940, tt. 17–23.

'Y Byd Helaethach', (The Life Abundant), *Y Drysorfa*, Cyf. Mai (May), 1940, tt. 166–71.

'Crefydd a Chymdeithas' (Religion and Society), *Y Cyfarwyddwr*, Cyf. XVII, Gorffennaf (July), 1940, tt. 202–4.

1941

'Dilema'r Prifysgol' (The Dilemma of the University), *Y Llenor*, Cyf. XX, Ebrill (April), 1941, tt. 31–42.

'Duw a'r Argyfyngau' (God and the Crisis), *Y Goleuad*, 16, 23 a 30
  Gorffennaf a 6 Awst (July and August), 1941, tt. 4–5, 4–5, 4–5, 4–5.
'Y Brifysgol a'r Werin' (The University and the People), *Transactions
  of the Honourable Society of Cymmrydorion*, 1941, pp. 40–70.
Crist a Gwleidyddiaeth (Christ and Politics), Pamffledi Heddychwyr
  Cymru, 11, Dinbych, Gwasg Gee, 1942.

1942

' "Self-satisfaction" and the "True Good" in Green's Moral Theory',
  Proceedings of the Aristotelian Society, Vol. XLII, 1942, pp. 151–82.
Adolygiad (Review) o W.T. Jones, *Mortality and Freedom*, yn *Efrydiau
  Athronyddol*, Cyf. V, 1942, tt. 47–50.

1943

Y Wladwriaeth a'i Hawdurdod (The State and its Authority), ynghyd â
  J.A. Thomas, Caerdydd, Gwasg Prifysgol Cymru, 1943.
Ebyrth a Cherddi Eraill (Sacrifices and other poems), Aberystwyth,
  Gwasg Aberystwyth, 1943.

1944

'The New Order: Personality and the New Order', *Expository Times*,
  Vol. LV, May 1944, pp. 200–3.
'Efengyl Y Cymod' (The Gospel of Reconciliation), *Sylfeini*, Cyf. 2,
  1944, tt. 167–72.
Adolygiad (Review) o A Peel, *The Christian Basis of Democracy*, yn
  Traethodydd, Cyf. XCIX, Gorffennaf (July) 1944, tt. 142–3.
Sylfeini Heddwch (The Foundations of Peace), golygwyd gan Simon B.
  Jones ac E. Lewis Evans, Cymdeithas Annibynwyr Cymraeg, 1944.

1945

Diogelu Diwylliant ac Ysgrifau Eraill (Safeguarding Culture), Gwasg Y
  Brython, 1945.
'Obedience to Conscience', *Mind*, Vol. LIV, July 1945, pp. 227–53.
Review of O.C. Quick, *The Gospel of the New World*, in *Mind* Vol. LIV,
  April 1945, pp. 182–3.
Adolygiad (Review) o Alwyn D. Rees, *Sylfeini Gweriniaeth* (Founda-
  tions of Democracy) yn *Efrydiau Athronyddol*, Cyf. VIII, 1945, t. 47.

1946

'The Authority of Conscience', *Congregational Quarterly*, Vol. XXIV, January 1946, pp. 41–7.

'On Poetic Truth', *Philosophy*, Vol. XXI, July 1946, pp. 147–66.

'Y Farddoniaeth Dywyll' (Obscure Poetry), *Y Drysorfa*, Cyf. CXVI, Awst (August), 1946, tt. 167–8.

Review of J.C. Flugel, *Man, Morals and Society in Mind*, Vol. LV, January 1946, pp. 83–5.

Review of Perelman, *De La Justice* in *Mind*, Vol. LV, 1946, p. 278.

Review of Martin Johnson, *Art and Scientific Thought*, in *Philosophy*, Vol. XXI, July 1946, pp. 167–8.

Review of P.A. Reid, *The Rediscovery of Belief*, in *Mind*, Vol. LV, October 1946, pp. 370–72.

1947

Morals and the New Theology, London, Gollancz and Harper, USA, 1947, p. 160.

Crist a Heddwch (Christ and Peace), Gwasg Gee, 1947.

'Conscience and Dissent', *Congregational Quarterly*, Vol. XXV, January 1947, pp. 47–55.

'Moral Freedom in Recent Ethics', *Proceedings of the Aristotelian Society*, Vol. XLVII, 1946–7, pp. 1–26.

'The Problem of Guilt', *Proceedings of the Aristotelian Society*, Supp. Vol. XXI 1947, pp. 175–96.

'Greek Ethics and Freedom', *Analysis*, Vol. 8, December 1947, pp. 17–23.

'Argyfwng a Datguddiad' (Crisis and Revelation), *Efrydiau Athronyddol*, Cyf. X, 1947, tt. 9–21.

Review of John Buffy, *A Philosophy of Poetry* Based on Thomistic Principles, in *Philosophy*, Vol. XXII, July 1947, pp. 167–8.

Review of B. Croce, *Politics and Morals* in *Mind*, Vol. XVI, 1947, pp. 176–7.

1948

'Collective Responsibility', *Philosophy*, Vol. XXIII, January 1948, pp. 3–18.

'Does the Good Will Define its own Content? — Study of T.H. Green's *Prolegomena to Ethics*', *Ethics*, Vol. LVIII, April 1948, pp. 157–79.

'Revelation and Reason', *Hibbert Journal*, Vol. XLVII, October 1948, pp. 56–64.

'Crefydd ac Argyfwng — (I)' (Religion and Crisis), *Eugrawn*, Cyf. CXL, Rhif 1, Ionawr (January), 1948, tt. 11–16.

'Nodyn: Cynhadledd Athronyddol, Harlech' (Note: Harlech Philosophical Conference), 31 Awst–2 Medi 1948 (31 August–2 September 1948), *Efrydiau Athronyddol*, Cyf. XI, 1948, t. 59.

'Crefydd ac Argyfwng — (2)' (Religion and Crisis), *Eurgrawn*, Cyf. CXL, Rhif 2, Chwefror (February), 1948, tt. 38–43.

'Arwyddion yr Amserau' (The Signs of the Times), *Y Drysorfa*, Llyfr CXVIII, Rhif 1340, 1948, tt. 153–6.

Review of Viscount Samuel, *Creative Men* in *Philosophy*, Vol. XXIII, January 1948, pp. 83–4.

Review of R.B. Perry, *Puritanism and Democracy* in *Mind*, Vol. LVII, July 1948, pp. 389–92.

1949

'Revelation and Art', Presidential Address to the Aristotelian Society, *Proceedings of the Aristotelian Society*, Supp. Vol. XXIII, 1949, pp. 1–30.

'Morality and Religion', *Philosophy*, Vol. XXIV, January 1949, pp. 34–55.

'Moral Autonomy and Freedom', *Hibbert Journal*, Vol. XLVII, July 1949, pp. 350–5.

'Mudiad Cristnogol y Myfyrwyr' (The Student Christian Movement), *Y Traethodydd*, Cyf. XVII, Gorffennaf (July) 1949, tt. 124–7.

'Dilyn Di Myfi' (Follow Thou Me), *Adroddiad Cyfarfodydd Undeb Yr Annibynwyr Cymraeg*, 1949, tt. 68–76.

Review of Urbin Edman, *Philosopher's Quest* in *Philosophy*, Vol. XXIV, July 1949, pp. 272–3.

1950

'Revelation without Content', *Hibbert Journal*, Vol. XLVIII, 1950, p. 379–382.

'The Present State of Ethics' *Cambridge Journal*, Vol. 3, No. 5, February 1950, pp. 259–76.

'Crisis and the Christian', *Congregational Quarterly*, Vol. XXVIII, January 1950, pp. 12–21.

'Education for the Ministry', *Welsh Anvil*, Vol. 2, August, 1950, pp. 53–70.

'The Theology of Reinhold Niebuhr', *Transactions of the Victoria Institute of Philosophy*, Vol. LXXXII, 1950, pp. 193–221.

Review of Lan Freed, *Social Pragmatism* in *Philosophy*, Vol. XXV, April 1950, pp. 183–5.

1951

Morals and Revelation, London, Allen and Unwin, 1951.

Dilyn Crist (Following Christ), Bangor, Jarvis and Foster, 1951.

Sosialaeth Bur, Anerchiad a draddodwyd i Undeb Charelwyr Gogledd Cymru yng Ngwyl Undeb y Chwarelwyr ym Mlaenau Ffestiniog, 7 Mai 1951, (Pure Socialism, a lecture delivered to the North Wales Quarrymen's Union in the Union of Quarrymen's Festival at Blaenau Ffestiniog, 7 May 1951), Caernarfon, Llyfrau'r Methodistiaid Calfinaidd, 1951.

'Trin yr Ardd' (Cultivating the Garden), *Y Genhinen*, Cyf. 1 Rhif 3, Haf (Summer), 1951, tt. 157–60.

'Cynhadledd Athronyddol Harlech', (The Harlech Philosophical Conference), *Efrydiau Athronyddol*, Cyf. XIII, tt. 37–8.

Review of Corliss Lamont *Humanism as a Philosophy* in *Philosophical Quarterly*, Vol. I, January 1951, p. 189.

Review of Paul Weiss, *Man's Freedom. A Philosopher offers the approach towards the good life for man*, in *Philosophy*, Vol. XXVII, 1951, pp. 280–3.

Review of H.G. Robinson, *Faith and Duty*, in *Philosophy*, Vol. XXVI, July 1951, pp. 277–80.

1952

Gwybod am Dduw: cip ar rai tueddiadau yn athroniaeth crefydd (Knowing about God: some trends in the philosophy of religion), Caerdydd, Gwasg Prifysgol Cymru, 1952.

'Impressions of a Present Question Conference'. *Journal of Education*, Vol. 84, November 1952, pp. 504–6.

'Revelation, Inspiration and Faith', *Modern Churchman*, Vol. XLII, September 1952, pp. 239–51.

'Individualism and Collectivism: A Study of T.H. Green's Ethics', *Ethics*, Vol. LXIII, October 1952, pp. 44–63.

'Religion and Mystery', *Congregational Quarterly*, Vol. XXX, January 1952, pp. 22–31.

'Freedom and Responsibility as the Moral Philosopher sees it', *Question*, Spring 1952, pp. 110–38.

'This Historical Element in the Gospel — A Discussion of Emil Brunner', *Theology*, Vol. LV, No. 384, June 1952, pp. 221–5.

'What is Theology?', *Philosophy*, Vol. XXVII, October 1952, pp. 345–58.

1953

'Private and Public Space', *Proceedings of the Aristotelian Society*, Vol. LIII, 1952/53, pp. 79–94.
'God and Nature', *Philosophy*, Vol. XXXVIII, April 1953, pp. 164–71.
'The Position of Philosophy in the University of Wales', *UNESCO: The Teaching of Philosophy — International Enquiry*, 1953, pp. 137–41.
'Y Ffydd sy'n Ymofyn' (The Faith that Seeks) in *Henry Jones 1852–1922*. Centenary Addresses delivered at the University College of North Wales, December 1952, edited by Hywel D. Lewis and Huw Morris-Jones, Caerdydd, Gwasg Prifysgol Cymru, 1953.
Review of A.C. Ewing, *The Fundamental Questions of Philosophy* in *Philosophy*, Vol. XXVIII, January 1953, pp. 88–91.
Review of Wilbur Marshall Urban, *Humanity and Deity* in *Mind*, Vol. LXII, April 1953, pp. 273–5.
Review of W.T. Stace, *Religion and the Modern Mind* in *Philosophy*, Vol. XXVIII, October 1953, pp. 374–6.

1954

'Survey of the Philosophy of Religion, 1945–52 — (I)', *Philosophical Quarterly*, Vol. IV, April 1954, pp. 166–81.
'Survey of the Philosophy of Religion, 1945–52 — (2)', *Philosophical Quarterly*, Vol. IV, July 1954, pp. 262–74.
'Christian Obedience' in *Studies in Christian Social Commitment*, ed. John Ferguson, London, 1954, pp. 108–26.
Review of David Wesley, *Major Voices in American Theology*, in *Hibbert Journal*, Vol. LIII, October 1954, pp. 85–6.

1955

'The Cognitive Factor in Religious Experience', *Proceedings of the Aristotelian Society*, Supp. Vol. XXIX, 1955, pp. 59–84.
'The Moral Status of Man', *Modern Churchman*, Vol. XLV, September 1955, pp. 232–46.
'The Present Relations between Religion and Science: An Introductory Note', *Hibbert Journal*, Vol. LIV, 1955/56, p. 1.
Review of Viscount Samuel *Belief and Action*, in *Philosophy*, Vol. XXX, April 1955, p. 187.
Review of R.S. Peters, *Brett's History of Psychology* in *Philosophy*, Vol. XXX, 1955, p. 88.
Review of D.H. Monro *Godwin's Moral Philosophy* in *Philosophy*, Vol. XXX, January 1955, pp. 89–90.

Reviews of Johannes Haklenberg, *Søren Kierkegaard* (trans. T.H. Croxall) and Michael Wishgorod, *Kierkegaard and Heidegger* in *Philosophy*, Vol. XXX, 1955, pp. 367–89.

1956

Editor. *Contemporary Moral Philosophy*, Vol. 3, Muirhead Library of Philosophy, London, Allen and Unwin, 1956.

'Worship and Idolatry' in *Contemporary British Philosophy*, Vol. 3, Muirhead Library of Philosophy, ed. H.D. Lewis, London, Allen and Unwin, 1956, pp. 263–86.

Review of C.A. Coulson, *Science and Religion: A Changing Relationship, The Rede Lecture for 1954*, in *Philosophy*, Vol. XXXI, 1956, pp. 279–80.

Review of A.C. Garnett, *Religion and the Moral Life*, in *Philosophy* Vol. XXXI, 1956, pp. 370–1.

Review of Sydney Spencer, *The Deep Things of God. Essays in Liberal Religion* in *Philosophy*, Vol. XXXI, 1956, pp. 373–4.

1957

'Faith and Freedom', *Theology*, Vol. LX, No. 444, June 1957, pp. 236–42.

'Contemporary Empiricism and the Philosophy of Religion', *Philosophy*, Vol. XXXII, July 1957, pp. 193–205.

'Dehongli Plato' (Interpreting Plato), *Efrydiau Athronyddol*, Cyf. 20, 1957, tt. 33–50.

1958

'The Autonomy of Ethics', *Proceedings of the Aristotelian Society*, Supp. Vol. XXXII, 1958, pp. 49–74.

1959

Our Experience of God, London, Allen and Unwin, 1959.

1960

'Our Experience of God'. H.D. Lewis and David Jenkins discuss Intuition, Evidence and Belief, *The Listener*, May 1960, pp. 884–5.

'Imagination and Experience' in *Metaphor and Symbol*, Proceedings of the Twelfth Symposium of the Colston Research Society, 1960, pp. 64–77.

1961

'Current Attenuations of Faith', *The Listener*, 23 February 1961, pp. 354–5.
'Mysterious Godhead', *The Listener*, 9 March 1961, pp. 434–5.
'Buddha and God', *The Listener*, 6 April 1961, pp. 616–17.
'Legal and Moral Responsibility', *The Listener*, 26 October 1961, pp. 645–6.
'Events and Dispositions', *The Philosophical Forum*, Vol. XVIII, 1961, pp. 3–21.
'God and Mystery' in *Prospect for Metaphysics*, ed. I.T. Ramsey, London, 1961, pp. 206–37.
'Freedom and Immortality', *Hibbert Journal*, January 1961, Vol. LIX, pp. 168–77.
Review of A.C. Ewing, *Second Thoughts in Moral Philosophy*, in *Philosophy*, Vol. XXXVI, 1961, pp. 234–6.
Review of *Essays in Unitarian Theology. A Symposium* edited by Kenneth Twinn, in *The Hibbert Journal*, Vol. LVIX, 1959/60, pp. 311–13.

1962

Freedom and History, London, Allen and Unwin, 1962.
'Schleiermacher — On Religion', *Theology*, Vol. 65, No. 501, March 1962, pp. 104–10.
'Responsibility and Mental Health', *Philosophy*, Vol. XXXVII, April 1962, pp. 165–75.
'Can History be Objective?' *International Philosophical Quarterly*, Vol. 11, No. 2, May 1962, pp. 219–43.
Review of Stephen Findlay, *Immortal Longings*, in *Hibbert Journal*, Vol. LX, 1961/62, pp. 173–5.
Review of Frederick Ferré, *Language, Logic and God* (New York, 1961) in *International Philosophical Quarterly*, Vol. 11, No. 2, May 1962, pp. 337–8.

1963

Editor, *Clarity is not Enough*, London, Allen and Unwin, 1963.
'Mind and Body — Some Observations on Mr. Strawson's Views',

Presidential Address to the Aristotelian Society, *Proceedings of the Aristotelian Society*, Vol. LXIII, 1962/63, pp. 1–22.
'Evangelism and Conversion', *Light and Salt Periodical*, Spring, 1963, pp. 315–34.
'Buddha and God', *The Monist*, Vol. 47, 1963, pp. 315–34.

1964

'Mysticism', *London Quaterly and Holborn Review*, Vol. CLXXXIX, July 1964, pp. 190–7.

1965

The Philosophy of Religion, Teach Yourself Series, London, English Universities Press, 1965.
'The Idea of Creation and Conceptions of Salvation', in *The Saviour God*, ed. S.G.F. Brandon, London, 1963, pp. 97–116.
'Beirniadu'r Grefydd Anghrediniol' (A Criticism of the Religion of Disbelief), (*Yr Argyfwng Gwacter Ystyr* gan J.R. Jones). Ymdriniaeth (Discussion). *Barn*, 27, 1965, tt. 71–2.

1966

With R.L. Slater, *World Religions*, London, C.A. Watts and Penguin, 1966.

1967

'Guilt', *Encyclopaedia of Philosophy*, ed. Paul Edwards, London, 1967, Vol. 3, pp. 395–7.
'History of the Philosophy of Religion', *Encyclopaedia of Philosophy*, ed. Paul Edwards, London, 1967, Vol. 6, pp. 276–85.

1968

Dreaming and Experience, London, Athlone Press, 1986.

1969

The Elusive Mind, Gifford Lectures at the University of Edinburgh, 1966–68, London, Allen and Unwin, 1969.

'Christian Belief Today, 1.2.3.4.', *The Times*, 12 and 26 April, 10 May, 14 June 1969.
'Sin and Salvation', *Dictionary of the History of Ideas*, November 1969, pp. 149–70.
'The Elusive Self and the I-Thou Relation' in *Talk of God*, ed. G.N.A. Vesey, Royal Institute of Philosophy Lecture Series 2, London Macmillan, 1969, pp. 168–84.
'Pa Beth yw Dyn?' (What is Man?) *Efrydiau Athronyddol*, Cyf. XXXII, 1969, tt. 26–42.

1970

The Elusive Mind, Muirhead Library of Philosophy, London, Allen and Unwin, 1970.
'Philosophy and Freedom of Conciousness', *Philosophy: Theory and Practice*, Proceedings of the International Seminar on World Philosophy, Madras, 1970, pp. 1–3.
'The Elusive Self and Practice', *Philosophy: Theory and Practice*, Proceedings of the International Seminar on World Philosophy, Madras, 1970, pp. 22–31.
'Edwards, David Miall (1873–1941)', *Y Bywgraffiadur Cymreig, 1941–1950*, Llundain, 1970, tt. 12–13.
Adolygiad (Review) o R.W. Beardsmore, *Moral Reasoning*, yn *Efrydiau Athronyddol*, Cyf. XXXIII, 1970, t. 77.

1971

Hen a Newydd: Argraffiadau o Daith i India (Old and New: Impressions of a Trip to India), Caernarfon, Llyfrau'r Methodistiaid Calfinaidd, 1971.
'Reflections on the Crisis of Christianity in India', *The Times*, 24 July 1971, p. 14.
Review of R.S. Downie and Elizabeth Telfer, *Respect for Persons*, in *Philosophy*, Vol. XLVII, 1971, pp. 282–3.

1972

'The Non-Moral Notion of Collective Responsibility' in *Individual and Collective Responsibility*, ed Peter A. French, New York, Schenkman Publishing Co., 1972, pp. 121–44.
Review of C.W.K. Mundle, *A Critique of Linguistic Philosophy*, in *Mind*, Vol. LXXXI, 1972, pp. 303–6.

1973

The Self and Immortality, London, Macmillan and Seabury Press, USA, 1973.

'A Study of the Notion of Life after Death in Contemporary Theology and Philosophy', in *Death in a Secular City*, ed. Russell Aldwinkle, London, Allen and Unwin, 1973, pp. 9–12.

'Responsibility of the Absolute Choice' in *Modern Introduction to Philosophy*, ed. Paul Edwards and Arthur Pap, New York, Free Press, 1973, pp. 47–51.

'Christology Today', *The Modern Free Churchman*, No. 97, 1973, pp. 6–12.

Paul Tillich, ed. Alistair Macleod, London, Allen and Unwin, 1973, in series *Contemporary Religious Thinkers*, advised by Hywel D. Lewis.

'Freedom and Immortality' in *Christian Empiricism*, ed. I.T. Ramsey, London, Sheldon Press, 1974, pp. 207–23.

'Realism and Metaphysics', *Idealistic Studies*, Vol. 4, No. 3, September 1974, pp. 208–23.

'Theism', *Encyclopaedia*, 1974, pp. 265–9.

'Gwybod a Bod yn Sicr' (Knowledge and Certainty), *Efrydiau Athronyddol*, Cyf. XXXVI, 1973, tt. 53–9.

1974

'Tribute to Professor Charles Arthur Campell', *The Times*, 20 March 1974, p. 18.

1975

'Survival', *Proceedings of the Aristotelian Society*, Supp. Vol. XLIX, 1975, pp. 211–30.

'Religion and the Paranormal' in *Philosophy and Psychical Research*, ed. S.C. Thakur, London, Allen and Unwin, Muirhead Library of Philosophy, pp. 142–55.

'Life after Death: H.D. Lewis argues the case with Anthony Quinton and Bernard Williams', *The Listener*, 9 August 1975, pp. 15–17.

'Belief in the Life Hereafter', *The Epworth Review*, Vol. 2, September 1975, pp. 95–101.

'The Belief in Life After Death' Drew Memorial Lecture, in *Contemporary Studies in Philosophical Idealism*, ed. John Howie and Thomas Burford, Boston, Stark and Co., 1975, pp. 149–60.

'The Elusive Self and Practice' in *The Personal Universe*, ed. T.E. Wren, London, Humanities Press, 1975, pp. 64–73.

'Editorial Notes', *Religious Studies*, Vol. 11, 1975, pp. 129–34.
'Credaf' (I Believe), *Barn*, Mehefin (June), 1975, tt. 683–4.
'The Study of Religion in the Universities' in *The Dynamics of Education* eds. G.R. Damodavan and H.D. Lewis, pp. 149–54.
'Y Gred mewn Anfarwoldeb' (The Belief in Immortality), *Efrydiau Athronyddol*, Cyf. XXXVIII, 1975, tt. 3–17.
'Er Cof; Yr Athro C.A. Campbell (In Memory; Professor C.A. Campbell), *Y. Bangoriad*, Cyf. 3/3, 1975, tt. 56–8.
'A Boom Period for Learning about Religion', *Times Higher Education Supplement*, 19 September 1975, p. 9.

1976

Editor, *Contemporary British Philosophy*. Muirhead Library of Philosophy. Vol. 4, London, Allen and Unwin, 1976.
Editor, *Philosophy East and West, Essays in Honour of Dr. T.M.P. Mahadevan*, London, Luzac and Co, 1976.
'Immortality and Dualism' in *Reason and Religion*, Royal Institute of Philosophy Symposium, ed. Stuart C. Brown, Cornell University Press, 1976, pp. 282–300.
'Pwy yw Iesu Grist?' (Who is Jesus Christ?), *Y. Traethodydd*, Cyf. 131, 1976, tt. 191–208.
Review of F.C. Copleston, *Religion and Philosophy* in *Heythrop Journal*, Vol. 17, No. 1, January 1976, pp. 68–71.

1977

'Ultimates and a Way of Looking in Philosophy' in *Contemporary Aspects of Philosophy* ed. Gilbert Ryle, London, Oriel Press, 1977, pp. 284–300.
'Persons and Recent Thought', in *The Search for Absolute Values in a Changing World*, Proceedings of the Sixth International Conference on the Unity of the Sciences, San Francisco, 1977, pp. 249–58.
'Theology and Ideology' in *Melanges Offerts au Henri Corbin*, Tehran, Offset Press, 1977, pp. 651–63.
'Heddiw nid Yfory' (Today, Not Tomorrow), *Y Faner*, 23 Rhagfyr (December) 1977, tt. 6–8.
'Ar Fryniau Kasia' (On Kasi Hills), *Y Goleuad*, 27 Ebrill (April) 1977, t. 1, 5.
'Y Cynhulliad a'r Brifysgol' (The Assembly and the University), *Y Faner*, Awst (August), 1977, tt. 18–19.
'Pwy yw Iesu Grist a Beth yw ei Bwysigrwydd i ni? (Who is Jesus Christ and what his significance for us?) yn *Nesau at Dduw*, gol.

(edited) Gwilym Arthur Jones, Llyfrau'r Methodistiaid Calfinaidd, 1977, tt. 33–6.
'Gwarchod Pawb' (The Part we all have to play in Culture), *Y Faner*, Mai (May), 1977.

1978

Persons and Life after Death, Library of Philosophy and Religion, London, Macmillan, 1978.
'Freedom and Authority in Rousseau', *Philosophy*, Vol. 53, 1978, pp. 353–62.
'Penodiadau ein Prifysgol' (University Appointments), *Barn*, 184, Mai (May), 1978, tt. 163–4.
'Ein Ffydd a'r Genhadaeth' (Faith and Mission), *Y Traethodydd*, Cyf. 133, Chwefror (February) 1978, tt. 135–47.
'Silver Fish'. Review of *The Sound of Wings*, Margaret Chatterjee, in *Christian Century*, November 1978, pp. 11138–9.
Review of Betty Shapin and Lissette Coly, editors, *The Philosophy of Parapsychology* in *The Christian Parapsychologist*, Vol. 3, No. 1, 1978, pp. 22–3.

1979

Pwy yw Iesu Crist? (Who is Jesus Christ?) Dinbych (Denbigh), Gwasg Gee, 1979.
'The Meaning of History' in *Logic, Ontology and Action*, edited D.P. Chattopadhyaya and P.K. Sen, India, Macmillan of India, 1979, pp. 1–14.
Review of *The Later Poetry of R.S. Thomas*, in *Poetry Wales*, Spring 1979, pp. 26–30.
'Llys heb Awdurdod' (A Court without Authority), *Y Faner*, 11 Mai (May), 1979, t. 8.
'Reply to Professor Bertocci', *Religious Studies*, Vol. XV, September 1979, pp. 407–9.
'Yng Ngwlad Pwyl' (In Poland), *Porfeydd*, Cyf. 2, Ionawr/Chwefror (January/February) 1979, tt. 3–6.
'Agoryd y Trysorau' (Opening the Treasures), *Y Faner*, 20 Gorffennaf (July), 1979, t. 7.
'Y Brifysgol a'r Gymru Gyfoes' (The University and Contemporary Wales), Darlith Rhydyfelen 1978, *Barn*, Rhagfyr/Ionawr (December/January), 1978/79, tt. 458–64.

1980

'Religious Experience' in *Experience, Reason and God*, ed. Eugene Thomas Long, Washington D.C., Catholic University of America Press, 1980, pp. 19–32.

'Fel y dangosodd y Refferendum, rhaid i ni fel Cymru . . .' (As the Referendum revealed, we must as Welshmen . . .), *Y Traethodydd*, Cyf. CXXXV, Ionawr (January) 1980, tt. 13–17.

1981

Jesus in the Faith of Christians, London Macmillan and India, 1981.

'Crist a Dioddefaint' (Christ and Suffering), *Y Traethodydd* Cyf. CXXXVI, Gorffennaf (July), 1981, tt. 136–48.

1982

The Elusive Self, Gifford Lectures at Edinburgh, Vol. 2. London, Macmillan and Edinburgh, 1982.

'Persons in Recent Thought' in *Mind and Brain*, ed. Sir John Eccles, Washington D.C., Paragon House, 1982, pp. 317–26.

'The Elusive Self' in *L'Heritage de Kant*, Melanges Philosophiques Offerts Au P. Marcel Regnier, Paris, 1982, pp. 397–412.

'O'Shaughnessy on Mind and Body', *Religious Studies*, Vol. 18, 1982, pp. 389–97.

'Aberthu'r Gymraeg mewn Coleg' (Sacrificing the Welsh Language in a College), *Y Faner*, 11 Mehefin (June) 1982, t. 3.

'Pa Beth yw Dyn?' (What is Man?), *Efrydiau Athronyddol*, Cyf. XLV, 1982, tt. 7–31.

1983

'The Logical Limits of Willing' *Mind*, Vol. XCII, October 1983, pp. 585–9.

'The Philosophy of Brand Blanshard', *Philosophy*, Vol. 58, 1983, pp. 110–17.

Review of I.M. Greengarten, *Thomas Hill Green and the Development of Liberal-Democratic Thought*, London, University of Toronto Press, 1981, in *Journal of the History of Philosophy*, Vol. XXI, No. 3, 1983, pp. 411–12.

'G.E. Moore', *The Times*, 17 November 1983, p. 13.

1984

'The British Idealists' in *Nineteenth Century Religious Thought in the West*, ed. Patrick Sherry and Ninian Smart, Cambridge University Press, 1984, Vol. 2, pp. 271–314.

'Solitude in Philosophy and Literature. The H.B. Acton Memorial Lecture' in *Philosophy and Literature* Royal Institute of Philosophy Lecture Series 16, ed. A Phillips Griffiths, Cambridge University Press, 1984, pp. 1–14.

'Lle'r Deall mewn Crefydd' (The Role of Understanding in Religion), yn *Y Meddwl Cyfoes*, Gol. Meredydd Evans, Caerdydd, Gwasg Prifysgol Cymru, 1984, tt. 10–17.

'Jesus and the Elusive Self' in *Philosophers on Their Own Work* (*Philosophes critiques d'eux memes*) Vol. XI, 1984, pp. 129–65.

'The Sword of Damocles or Christ', *Theology*, Vol. LXXXVII, January 1984, pp. 3–6.

1985

Freedom and Alienation, Gifford Lectures, Vol. 3, Edinburgh, Scottish Academic Press, 1985.

'The Distinctness of Persons' in *Studies in the Philosophy of J.N. Findlay*, edited Robert S. Cohen, Richard M. Martin, and Merold Westphal, State University of New York Press, 1985, pp. 377–94.

'Immortality' in *Review and Expositor* (Baptist Theological Journal), Vol. LXXXII, No. 4, 1985, pp. 549–63.

'Commentary': J. Beloff, *Parapsychology and Radical Dualism*, in *Journal of Religion and Psychical Research*, Vol. 8, January 1985, pp. 45–51.

1986

'Elfennau Sylfaenol ein Ffydd' (The Essential Elements of our Faith) yn *Y Gair a'r Genedl* Cyfrol Deyrnged i R. Tudur Jones, Golygydd E. Stanley John, Abertawe, Ty John Penri, 1986, tt. 226–37.

1988

Gofidiau Patsi: Cerddi Ysgafn (The Worries of Patsi: light-hearted poems). Gwasg Gee. 1988.

Llythyr: 'Trafod Ffilm' (Discussing the film, 'The Last Temptation of Christ'). *Y Faner*, 23 Medi (September) 1988, t. 18.

Index

List of Subscribers

The following have associated themselves with the publication of this volume through subscription:

Andrew P. Adams, Worcester Park, Surrey
Russell Aldwinckle, McMaster University, Canada
Ian W. Alexander, University College of North Wales, Bangor
Violaine Arès, Montreal
A. MacC. Armstrong, Malvern
Meshack Y. Asare, London
Robin Attfield, Cardiff
Paul Badham, St. David's University College, Lampeter
Paul H. Ballard, University of Wales College of Cardiff
Renford Bambrough, St. John's College, Cambridge
W.H.F. Barnes, Edinburgh
Richard H. Bell, The College of Wooster, USA
Fred Berthold Jr., Dartmouth College, USA
J.G. Bishop, Dartington
Gordon Blackford, Manchester
Beryl Bowskill, Mundesley, Norfolk
Vincent Brümmer, Utrecht
Fernand Brunner, Cortaillod, Switzerland
Gerd Buchdahl, Cambridge
Thomas O. Buford, Furman University, USA
John Ross Carter, Colgate University, USA
Venant Cauchy, Université de Montréal
Peter Caws, The George Washington University, USA
George D. Chryssides, Polytechnic South West, Plymouth
Thomas Clough Daffern, University of London
Dafydd G. Davies, Caerdydd

I.E. Davies, Port Talbot
Richard T. De George, University of Kansas
George M. De Santos, Beckenham, Kent
J.P. Dixon, Ashford, Middlesex
Peter Donovan, Massey University, New Zealand
James Nelson Dougan, London
Bohumil S. Drasar, London
George Dunseth, Wimborne, Dorset
John C. Eccles, Contra, Switzerland
Hywel a Gwen Evans, Conwy
J.D.G. Evans, Queen's University, Belfast
Owen E. Evans, University College of North Wales, Bangor
John Ferguson, Birmingham
Angela Jane Fineron, York
Carlos Avila Flores, Mexico City
Paul Gochet, University of Liège
Lourdes Gordillo, Universidad de Murcia
Carol G.M. Gray, London
Pete A.Y. Gunter, University of North Texas
Leila Haaparanta, University of Helsinki
M.G. Haddock, Newport
Earl of Halsbury, London
S.M. Hardwicke, Chorley Wood, Hertfordshire
Jonathan Harrison, Cambridge
Brian Hebblethwaite, Queens' College, Cambridge
David. C. Hicks, University of Aberdeen
Jaakko Hintikka and Ghita Holmstrom-Hintikka, Tallahassee,
    Florida
G.E. Hughes, Victoria University of Wellington, New Zealand
Geoffrey Hunter
Youn-Chan Ip, Vancouver
Grace Jantzen, King's College, London
Anders Jeffner, Uppsala University
Aneurin M. Jones, Aberteifi
Gerald E. Jones, Institute of Religion, Stanford, USA
Gwilym H. Jones, University College of North Wales, Bangor
Moses J. Jones, Yr Wyddgrug
O.R. Jones, Aberystwyth
R. Denis Jones, Porthaethwy
R. Tudur Jones, University College of North Wales, Bangor

T. Glanville Jones, Barry
Alec Kassman, London
Jacquelyn A. Kegley, California State University
Haig Khatchadourian, Milwaukee
Rosemarie Kieffer, Luxembourg
William and Martha Kneale, Skipton
Stephan Körner, Bristol
Jean-Yves Lacoste, Paris
Pat LeFeuvre, Chelmsford
Ramon M. Lemos, University of Miami
A. Marilyn Lewis, Pwllheli
Julius Lipner, Faculty of Divinity, Cambridge
Donald M. MacKinnon, Aberdeen
D.L.C. Maclachlan, Queen's University at Kingston
Brian Magee, Kings College, London
W. James Maginnis, Lisburn
Noël Mailloux, Montreal
Mohammed Maruf, Islamia College, Lahore
E. Gwynn Matthews, Llanrhaeadr-yng-Nghinmeirch
James McNicholas, Wellingborough
Samuel J. Mikolaski, Escondido, California
T.R. Miles, University College of North Wales, Bangor
Basil Mitchell, Oriel College, Oxford
Peter J. Mitchell, Hughes Hall, Cambridge
A.C. Montefiore, Balliol College, Oxford
Peggy Morgan, Westminster College, Oxford
Seyyed Hossein Nasr, George Washington University, USA
Stephen W. Need, The Theological College, Chichester
B.J. Nesfield-Cookson, Hawkwood College, Stroud
James Nicholas, Bangor
M.T. Ntumba, Düsseldorf
Matthew Ojei-Gyawu, London
Helen Oppenheimer, Jersey
Harry Owen, Gerrards Cross
Raimon Panikkar, Barcelona
W.A. de Pater, Katholieke Universiteit Leuven
Sir Karl Popper, CH, University of London
W. Eifion Powell, Caerdydd
R. Pring, University of Exeter
Mr and Mrs D.A. Rees, Jesus College, Oxford

D. Ben Rees, Liverpool
M. Régnier, Paris
Glyn Richards, University of Stirling
David H. Roberts, Durham
E ap Nefydd Roberts, United Theological College,
    Aberystwyth
J.O. Roberts, Benllech, Ynys Môn
J.W. Roberts, Eton College
Edwin H. Robertson, Hampstead
The Revd and Mrs J.H.L. Rowlands, St Michael's College,
    Llandaff
Edmund Runggaldier, University of Innsbruck
John Ryan, Llandrillo-yn-Rhos
Hermann H. Sallinger, Krumbach, Germany
Mario Sancipriano, Università di Siena
Bernard Shannon, Isle of Man
John Geoffrey Sharps, Scarborough
D.W.D. Shaw, University of St Andrews
Marcus G. Sims, Lichfield
W. Solomon, London
Christine Spahn, Nürnberg
D.M. Stanesby, Canon of Windsor
Sir Peter Strawson, Magdalen College, Oxford
Frank Suddards, Barmouth
D.O. Thomas, Aberystwyth
John Heywood Thomas, University of Nottingham
Eric Toms, Edinburgh
Martin C. Underwood, Reading
Bertel Wahlström, Katedralskolan i Åbo, Finland
Gilbert Walton, Keble College, Oxford
Gerald Joseph Wanjohi, University of Nairobi
Keith Ward, King's College, London
Martin Warner, University of Warwick
W.G. Webster, Dunblane
D.A. Whewell, University of Durham
Arthur a John Tudno Williams, Aberystwyth
Cyril G. Williams, Coleg Prifysgol Dewi Sant, Llanbedr
J. Gwynn Williams, Bangor
Stephen Nantlais Williams, Aberystwyth
W.I. Cynwil Williams, Eglwys y Crwys, Caerdydd

Anton Wills-Eve, West Kirby, Wirral
Kenneth Wilson, Westminster College, Oxford
John Wood, Walsham le Willows
Eric Woods, University of Bristol
Frances M. Young, University of Birmingham

Center of Metaphysics and Philosophy of God, University of
  Leuven
Coleg y Bedyddwyr, Bangor
Graduate Theological Union Library, Berkeley, California
Institute of Philosophy, University of Leuven
Ira J. Taylor Library, Iliff School of Theology, Denver
The Library, University of Edinburgh
New College Library, University of Edinburgh
The Royal Institute of Philosophy
Salisbury & Wells Theological College
Spurgeon's College, London
St Deiniol's Library, Hawarden
St Michael's College, Llandaff
Trinity College, Ghana
Tyndale House Library, Cambridge
Wesley College Library, Bristol
Westminster College, Cambridge